LINGUISTIC SURVEYS OF AFRICA

Volume 17

THE BANTU LANGUAGES OF AFRICA

THE BANTU LANGUAGES OF AFRICA
Handbook of African Languages

M. A. BRYAN

LONDON AND NEW YORK

First published in 1959 by Oxford University Press

This edition first published in 2018
by Routledge
2 Park Square, Milton Park, Abingdon, Oxon OX14 4RN

and by Routledge
711 Third Avenue, New York, NY 10017

Routledge is an imprint of the Taylor & Francis Group, an informa business

© 1959 International African Institute

All rights reserved. No part of this book may be reprinted or reproduced or utilised in any form or by any electronic, mechanical, or other means, now known or hereafter invented, including photocopying and recording, or in any information storage or retrieval system, without permission in writing from the publishers.

Trademark notice: Product or corporate names may be trademarks or registered trademarks, and are used only for identification and explanation without intent to infringe.

British Library Cataloguing in Publication Data
A catalogue record for this book is available from the British Library

ISBN: 978-1-138-08975-4 (Set)
ISBN: 978-1-315-10381-5 (Set) (ebk)
ISBN: 978-1-138-09710-0 (Volume 17) (hbk)
ISBN: 978-1-138-09791-9 (Volume 17) (pbk)
ISBN: 978-1-315-10495-9 (Volume 17) (ebk)

Publisher's Note
The publisher has gone to great lengths to ensure the quality of this reprint but points out that some imperfections in the original copies may be apparent.

Disclaimer
The publisher has made every effort to trace copyright holders and would welcome correspondence from those they have been unable to trace.

Due to modern production methods, it has not been possible to reproduce the fold-out maps within the book. Please visit www.routledge.com to view them.

THE
BANTU LANGUAGES
OF AFRICA

COMPILED BY

M. A. BRYAN

Published for the
INTERNATIONAL AFRICAN INSTITUTE
by the
OXFORD UNIVERSITY PRESS
LONDON   NEW YORK   CAPE TOWN
1959

Oxford University Press, Amen House, London E.C.4
GLASGOW NEW YORK TORONTO MELBOURNE WELLINGTON
BOMBAY CALCUTTA MADRAS KARACHI KUALA LUMPUR
CAPE TOWN IBADAN NAIROBI ACCRA

© *International African Institute 1959*

PRINTED IN GREAT BRITAIN

FOREWORD

THIS volume is the fourth and last part of the general survey of the languages of Africa which has been prepared and published by the International African Institute over the last six years under the title *Handbook of African Languages*. It was originally intended that the present volume should be compiled by Professor Malcolm Guthrie, head of the African Department of the School of Oriental and African Studies, University of London. Professor Guthrie, however, having assembled a considerable body of material, was prevented by pressure of other work from preparing it for publication. He therefore made his notes available to Miss M. A. Bryan, who was good enough to act as compiler, and, drawing on additional sources, has prepared this volume, the arrangement of which follows in the main that adopted in Parts II and III of the Handbook (*Languages of West Africa*; *Non-Bantu Languages of North-eastern Africa*).

The International African Institute, and the authors of the several parts of the Handbook, desire to express their thanks to the British Colonial Social Science Research Council for securing and administering the grant from Colonial Development and Welfare Funds which has enabled the *Handbook of African Languages* to be produced; to the Institute's Linguistic Advisory Committee which planned and supervised the work, and to the numerous scholars, research workers, and African informants who have most generously given help and advice.

Although the study of African languages has made notable progress in recent years, much still remains to be done. It is our hope that the *Handbook*, though inevitably tentative and incomplete, has made a solid contribution to this field of study and will provide a basis on which other scholars and students will be able to build.

DARYLL FORDE
Director, International African Institute

London, 1958

CONTENTS

Acknowledgements and Explanatory Notes	page ix
Lundu Group	1
Mbo Group	3
Duala Group	6
Bube Group	9
Basa Group	10
Bafia Group	13
'Sanaga' Group	14
Yaunde-Fang Group	16
Makaa Group	19
Kaka Group	22
Myene Single Unit	23
Kota Group	24
Tsogo Group?	25
Shira-Punu Group	26
Njabi Group	27
Mbete Group	28
Teke-Yans Group	29
Ngul Single Unit?	32
Ngando Group	33
Pande Group	34
Mboshi Group	36
Ngala Group	37
Ngombe Group	43
Kele Group	46
Mongo-Nkundo Group	48
Tetela Group	52
Kuba Group	54
Kongo Group or Single Unit	56
Kimbundu Single Unit	63
Samba-Holu Group?	65
Kwangali Single Unit	66
Chokwe-Lunda Group	67
Luyana Group	70
Luba Group	72
Nkoya Group	75
Fipa-Mambwe Group	76
Nyiha-Safwa Group	77
Nyakyusa Single Unit	79
Bemba Group	80
Ila Group	83
Totela Group?	85
Kari Group	86
Bali Group	88
Bira Group	89
Lega Group	92
Nande Group	95
Shi-Hunde Group	97
Ha Group	100
Nyali Group	101
Mbole-Ena Group?	103
Inter-Lacustrine Group	104
Gisu Group (or Single Unit?)	110
Luhya Group	111
Gusii Group	113
Kikuyu Group	115
Shaka (Chagga) Group	117
Tongwe Group?	118
Sukuma Group	119
Nilyamba Group	120
Gogo Group	121
Shambaa Group	122
Zaramo Group	123
Taita Group	125

CONTENTS

Swahili Group	126	Shona Group	143
Pogolo Group	130	Venda Single Unit	147
Hehe Group	131	Sotho-Tswana Group	148
Ngindo Group	133	Nguni Group	152
Yao Group	134	Tsonga Group	155
Makua Group	135	Chopi Group	157
Manda Group	136	Umbundu Group	158
Tumbuka Single Unit	137	Kuanyama Group	159
Nyanja Single Unit	139	Herero Single Unit	160
Nsenga Group	141	Yei Single Unit	160

ACKNOWLEDGEMENTS AND EXPLANATORY NOTES

The main sources used are:

MG1	GUTHRIE, *The Classification of the Bantu Languages* (1948).
MG2	GUTHRIE, *The Bantu Languages of Western Equatorial Africa* (1953).
MG3	GUTHRIE, Revised classified list of Bantu languages (MS.). This list supersedes the groupings and orthography of MG1 and MG2.
NBi, ii, iii	*Linguistic Survey of the Northern Bantu Borderland*, Vol. I, parts i, ii, iii (1956).
NBII	*Linguistic Survey of the Northern Bantu Borderland*, Vol. II.
DB	DOKE, *Bantu* (1945).
DSB	DOKE, *The Southern Bantu Languages* (1954).
VBRL	VAN BULCK, *Les Recherches linguistiques au Congo Belge* (1948).
H50	HULSTAERT, *Carte linguistique du Congo Belge* (1950).
H51	HULSTAERT, 'Les Langues de la cuvette centrale congolaise' (*Aequatoria*, 1951).
H54	HULSTAERT, *Au sujet de deux cartes linguistiques du Congo Belge* (1954).
IESC	DUGAST, *Inventaire ethnique du sud-Cameroun* (1949).
GA	ATKINS, personal communication.
EW	WESTPHAL, personal communication.

Other sources are acknowledged in footnotes.

A list of languages and dialects is given at the head of each Group. These lists are arranged in columns.

All columns except right hand: main sources quoted in the text (the fullest and/or most reliable source being placed in the left-hand column where possible).[1]

Right-hand column: alternative names or spellings of names which are or have been used in literature (in lower-case type); also, in some Groups, additional sources quoted in the text (in capitals).

The symbol † is used to indicate 'mixed' languages, i.e., those with affiliations with more than one Group.

Reference letters and numbers used in the sources quoted are given in the lists:

MG3: Zone letter and Group and language number. Note that these do not always correspond with those in MG1. Languages or dialects on which Guthrie has first-hand material are indicated by * following the reference number, other languages by o.

NBi: Numbers of units.

NBii: Geographical names of groups and letters and numbers of sub-groups, languages, &c. The following abbreviations are used: W., West; W.C., West Central; N., North; E., East; Extr., Extreme; Trans., Transition.

No attempt at orthographical consistency has been made; the spelling of any one name is generally that used by the authority quoted for that particular unit; where an accepted or official orthography is in use, this is also indicated.

[1] Where different sources are used for different parts of one Group, this arrangement is, of course, not possible (e.g. Inter-Lacustrine Group, p. 104).

Moreover, several different phonetic systems are used, so that the same symbol may have different values in different parts of the book.

VOWELS. The following symbols are used in MG3 and NBi and iii.

I̧	very close	Ɔ	semi-open
I	close or very close[1]	O	semi-close
Ȩ	close e	Ọ	close o
E	semi-close	U	close or very close[1]
Ɛ	semi-open	U̧	very close
A	fully open		

Ë, Ï, Ö   centralized (Ə is used in NBi instead of Ë)
Ɔ̃, &c. nasalized

The following phonetic symbols are also used:

ɒ	open ɔ
ʌ	as in English 'but'
ɪ, ʊ	open i and u

CONSONANTS. The phonetic values of the consonants are:

	Bilabial	Labio-dental	Dental	Alveolar	Post-alveolar	Lateral	Palatal	Velar	Labio-velar	Glottal
Explosive, unvoiced	p			t			c	k	kp	ʼ
unexploded								k̡		
aspirated	ph			th			ch	kh		
voiced	b		ḍ	d			ɉ	g	gb	
Implosive	ɓ			ɗ						
Nasal	m		ṇ	n			ny	ŋ		
Fricative, unvoiced	ƒ	f	θ	s	ʃ	ɬ		x		h
voiced	ʋ	v	ð	z, ʐ		ɮ		ɣ		
Affricate, unvoiced				ts	tʃ			kx		
aspirated						tɬh		kxh		
voiced				dz	dʒ					
Liquid				l						
Rolled				r						
Flapped				ɾ						
Semi-vowel	w						y, ẇ			
Nasal Compound	mb		ṇḍ	nd				ŋg		

The majority of the symbols used in this book correspond to the above. The main divergencies and variations are:

ɓ: B (MG3, NBi, iii, Doke); ʼB (NBii, VBRL)
ƒ: P (MG3, NBi, iii)

[1] In five-vowel languages, cedillas are not used.

ACKNOWLEDGEMENTS AND EXPLANATORY NOTES   xi

ʋ: B̠ (MG3, NBi, iii); V (DSB); Ŵ (DB)
θ: T̠H̠ (NBiii); TH (MG3)
ð: D̠ (MG3); DH (NBiii)
ɗ: D (MG3, NBi, iii); 'D (NBii, VBRL)
ʑ: ZW (DSB); ZV (New orthography, SHONA Group)
ɽ: L or R according to local convention (NBiii)
ʃ: SH (MG3, NBii, iii, VBRL, Doke); S̠ (NBi)
tʃ: C; CH
dʒ: J; DJ
ɬ: HL
tɬh: THL
ɫ: (nasalized) NDL
c: C; CH
ch: CH
j: J; DJ
ŋ: D; NG'
x: K̠ (MG3); X (NBiii, EW); G (Official orthography, SOTHO-TSWANA Group)
γ: G̠ (MG3, NBi, iii)
kx: KX (EW); KG (Official orthography, SOTHO-TSWANA Group)
kxh: KXH (EW); KG (Official orthography, SOTHO-TSWANA Group)
ŋg: DG; NG

Clicks are represented as follows:
  / (dental): C; voiced: GC
  ! (alveolar): Q; voiced nasal: G
  ǁ (lateral): X; aspirated: XH

Other abbreviations used:

TERRITORIAL

A.	Angola	O.-C.	Oubangui-Chari
B.C.	British Cameroons	O.F.S.	Orange Free State
B.P.	Bechuanaland Protectorate	P.E.A.	Portuguese East Africa
C.	Cameroun	R.-U.	Ruanda-Urundi
C.B.	Congo Belge	S.A.	Union of South Africa
G.	Gabon	S.R.	Southern Rhodesia
K.	Kenya	S.W.A.	South-West Africa
M.-C.	Moyen-Congo	T.T.	Tanganyika Territory
N.	Nyasaland	U.	Uganda
N.R.	Northern Rhodesia		

ADMINISTRATIVE

D.	District	Rég.	Région
Div.	Division	S.-D.	Sous-division
Prov.	Province	Terr.	Territoire

LUNDU GROUP

Where spoken: B.C.

	MG3	NBi		Other names
LUNDU	A.11:			
⎧LUNDU[1]	A.11a/o	LUNDU	1	Balundu
⎪NGƆRƆ	A.11b/o	ŊGƆRƆ	7	Ngolo
⎪BAKU̱NDU̱	A.11c/o	BAKUNDU	6	Lokundu, Kundu
⎨⎰BATANGA	A.11d/o	BATAŊGA	4	
⎪⎱BI̱MA		BI̱MA	5	
⎪⎰EKU̱MBƐ	A.11e/o	EKU̱MBƐ	2	
⎩⎱MBƆNGƐ		MBƆŊGƐ	3	
BARU̱Ɛ	A.12/o	BARU̱Ɛ	8	Lue, W. Kundu

LUNDU
Where spoken: Kumba Div., in almost the entire western part of the Division (the most westerly Bantu language).
Number: 6,234 (Talbot[2]—'probably very unreliable'—NBi).

NGƆRƆ
Where spoken: Kumba Div., on the heights and slopes of Rumpi hills.
Number: 5,837 (Talbot), perhaps including the BATANGA.

BAKU̱NDU̱
Where spoken: Kumba Div. (*a*) on the north-eastern slopes of Rumpi hills along 5° S.; (*b*) in an irregular-shaped patch south-west and south of Kumba.
Number: 5,010 (Talbot).
LOKUNDU is the name recorded by Bufe.[3] According to NBi, however, an informant insisted on BAKU̱NDU̱ as the linguistic, as well as the tribal, name. Vocabulary difference between NBi and Bufe's material suggests either an increase of foreign influence or the existence of more than one dialect.

BATANGA
Where spoken: Kumba Div., on the northern slopes of Rumpi hills, south of the divisional border.
Number: See under NGƆRƆ above.

BI̱MA, spoken by ba-IMA, formerly known as ba-UMA (NBi).
Where spoken: Kumba Div. (*a*) on the western and north-western slopes of Rumpi hills south of the divisional border; (*b*) in the BALUNDU-BAKU̱NDU̱ area extending westwards from Ndian into Nigeria.

---
[1] Exact quality of vowel not known (MG, personal communication).
[2] *The Peoples of Southern Nigeria* (1926).
[3] 'Die Dualasprache in ihrem Verhältnis zu den Dialekten des Nordgebiets der Station Bombe' (*Z.K.S.* 1910).

LUNDU GROUP

'BATAŊGA and BIMA are merely dialectal variants of one language' (NBi).

ƐKỤMBƐ

Where spoken: Kumba Div. (*a*) south of Kumba on both sides of the Kumba–Victoria road, and eastwards to the frontier; (*b*) 9° 10′ E., 4° 30′ N., and as far as the frontier.

Number: 844 (Talbot).

MBƆNGƐ

Where spoken: Kumba Div., on the south-eastern slopes of Rumpi hills almost to 9° E., 4° 30′ N.

Number: 6,107 (Talbot).

There are only 'dialectal differences' between ƐKỤMBƐ and MBƆDGƐ (NBi).

BARỤƐ

Where spoken: Kumba Div., on the southern slopes of Rumpi hills around the headwaters of R. Makunge and R. Meme.

Number: 4,733 (Talbot).

MBO GROUP

Where spoken: B.C., C.

	MG3		NBi		Other names
†BALOŊ	A.13/*	BALOŊ		21a	S. Balong, Balung
See also DUALA and BASA Groups, pp. 6, 10.					
†BƆNKĘŊ	A.14/*	BƆŊKƐŊ		21b	Bonkeng, Bonken Pendia

See also DUALA and BASA Groups.

MBO	A.15:				
⎧BAFƆ	A.15a/o	BAFƆ		17	Bafaw
		? BALƆNDƆ		18	Balondo
		? BABƆDG		19	Babong
⎪MBỌ	A.15g/o	MBỌ		20a–d	Ŋgɛn (20d), Bareko
		BANĘKA		20e	
⎪KAA	A.15f/o	KAA		20f	Bakaka
		MWAHƐT		20g	Manehas, Bakaka
		KƆƆSƏ[1] (a-)		20h	Muamenam, Mbo
⎨KƆƆSË (a-)	A.15b/o	KƆƆSƏ (a-)		20i	Bakosi, Bakossi, Nkosi
⎪SWASË (n-)	A.15c/o	SWƆSƏ (n-) (n-swɒsə)		20j	Basosi
⎪LÖŊ (e-)	A.15d/o	LÖŊ (e-) (llʌŋ)		20k	Elong
⎩NĘNŨ (n-)	A.15e/o	NĘNŨ (n-)		20l	Ninong

MG2 includes MBO with LUNDU, &c., in one Group, but says that 'this curious group of dialects . . . is in many respects in a category by itself owing to their peculiar phonology'.[2]

†BALOŊ

Where spoken: B.C., Victoria and Kumba Divisions, in a crescent-shaped area round the north-eastern slopes of Mt. Cameroon, extending as far as R. Mungo; C., Rég. Moungo, S.-D. Mbanga, on the left bank of R. Moungo (Mungo), extending east beyond Mbanga.

Number: B.C. 2,033 (Talbot), C. 2,406 (IESC).

BALOŊ 'shares some features with DUALA, MBO, and MBƐNƐ [BASA]' (NBi).

†BƆNKĘŊ

Where spoken: C., Rég. Moungo, in the north-western part of S.-D. Mbanga on both sides of the Loum–Nyombe road.

Number: 1,690 (IESC).

---

[1] In this Group there is a very central vowel, represented in MG3 by Ë and in NBi mostly by Ə.
[2] For further details, see NBi, pp. 22–23.

BƆNKƐD 'shows vocabulary resemblance with LƆMBI [BASA Group] and KAA [MBO Cluster]; it has many features of the MBƐNƐ [i.e. BASA] class system and some of MBO. Its word-shape, however, would point to a DUALA or LUNDU origin' (NBi).

BAFƆ

Where spoken: B.C., Kumba Div., (*a*) along the main road north from Kumba almost to the divisional border, (*b*) 9° 10' E., 4° 30' N.
Number: 2,397 (Talbot).
It is not certain whether BAFƆ should be considered as a dialect of the MBO Cluster or as a separate language within the Group.

? BALƆNDƆ (administrative name BALONDO)

Where spoken: C., S.-D. Nkongsamba, south of Mt. Nlonako.
Number: 263 (IESC).
Information on BALƆNDƆ is fragmentary; it is included here on the strength of statements by informants (NBi).

? BABƆDG (administrative name BABONG)

Where spoken: C., S.-D. Nkongsamba, 9° 55'–10° E., 4° 40'–4° 45' N.
Number: 1,217 (IESC).

MBO (*a*) 'British Cameroons MBO';
(*b*) MBỌ of Mbouroukou;
(*c*) MBỌ of Dschang;
(*d*) MBỌ (BAREKO).

Where spoken: (*a*) B.C., in the south-eastern part of Mamfe Div., extending into C. (*b*) C., in and around Mbouroukou chefferie, S.-D. Nkongsamba; (*c*) C., immediately south and south-west of Dschang, S.-D. Nkongsamba, extending in the north into B.C.; (*d*) C., north-east of Nkongsamba as far as R. Nkam.
Number: (*a*) 3,037 (Talbot); (*b*, *c*) 7,816 (IESC)+*c*. 3,000 in B.C.; (*d*) 2,752 (IESC).
(*a*) and (*b*) 'are sufficiently close together to be called dialects of the same language'; (*c*) has more striking divergencies (which are reminiscent of BAMILEKE), and some informants state that it is understood by other MBO-speakers with difficulty; (*d*) is said to be inter-intelligible with (*b*) and identical with the speech of the BANẸKA (see below) (NBi, II).

BANẸKA

Where spoken: C., in the Nkongsamba area.
Number: 2,961 (IESC).
See (*d*) above.

KAA

Where spoken: C., S.-D. Nkongsamba, 9° 40'–9° 58' E., 4° 35'–4° 50' N.
Number: 5,327 (IESC).

MBO GROUP

MWAHƐT (called BAKAKA by MBǪ informants)

Where spoken: C., S.-D. Nkongsamba, east of Mt. Koupé, extending to the Nkongsamba–Bonabéri road.
Number: 2,413 (IESC) (including 'some related foreigners').

KƆƆSƏ (a-)

Where spoken: C., S.-D. Nkongsamba, west of Nkongsamba on the international frontier, south of Mt. Manengouba.
Number: 1,844 (IESC).

KƆƆSË (NKOSI) (probably a dialectal variant of the above)

Where spoken: B.C., Kumba Div., on the heights and slopes of Mt. Manenguba (Manengouba), extending to the Cameroun border and perhaps beyond.

SWASË (n-)

Where spoken: B.C., Kumba Div., east of the Kumba–Mamfe road on the northwestern slopes of Mt. Manenguba, bounded in the north by the divisional boundary.
Number: c. 3,000 (NBII).

LÖƉ (e-)

Where spoken: B.C., Kumba Div., and C., S.-D. Nkongsamba, between 5° and 5° 15′ N.
Number: 3,803 (Talbot).

NƐNǓ (n-)

Where spoken: B.C., Kumba Div., and C., S.-D. Nkongsamba, around 5° N.
Number: 2,624 (Talbot).

DUALA GROUP

Where spoken: B.C., C.

MG3		NBi		Ardener[1]	Other names
B̠OMB̠OK̠O	A.21/o	B̠OMB̠OK̠O	10	MBOKO	Bamboko, Bambuku, Bomboko, Bumbuko
				BOB̠EA	Bobe, Bobea, Bota, Wovea
B̠AAKPE̠	A.22/o	MO̠KPE̠	11	MOKPE	Baakpe, Bakwiri, Kweli, Kwili, Kwiri
SU̠	A.23/o	SU̠((i)su̠)	12	ISU(WU)	Bimbia, Isubu, Subu
DU̠ALA	A.24/*			DUALA	Douala
				KƆLƐ	Bakolle
		BOD̠IMAN	16	BODIMAN	
O̠LI̠	A.25/*	O̠LI̠	13	OLI	Ewodi, Wouri, Wuri
⎰PO̠NGO̠	A.26/*	PO̠ŊGO̠	14	PONGO	
⎱MU̠NGO̠		MU̠ŊGO̠	15	MONGO	
MU̠LI̠MBA	A.27/*			LIMBA	Malimba
†(BALO̠Ŋ	A.13/*)	(BALOŊ	21a)		
See also MBO Group, p. 3.					
†(BƆNKEŊ	A.14/*)	(BƆŊKEŊ	21b)		
See MBO Group.					
		'S. BAKOKO'			
		†'N. BAKOKO'—see also BASA and YAUNDE-FANG Groups, pp. 10, 16.			

B̠OMB̠OK̠O

Where spoken: B.C., north and north-west of Mt. Cameroon, descending to the coast.
Number: c. 2,000 (Ardener).

BOB̠EA

Where spoken: B.C., Bota Island in the Pirate Group in Ambar Bay, and a village on the opposite coast (Ardener).
Number: 555 (Ardener).
Very closely related to B̠OMB̠OK̠O. The speakers are of BUBI origin, now assimilated to the KPE (Ardener).

MO̠KPE̠

Where spoken: B.C., on and around Mt. Cameroon, descending to the coast.
Number: 15,581+ (Ardener).
Has some affinities with the LUNDU and MBO Groups (Ardener).

[1] *Coastal Bantu of the Cameroons* (Eth. Survey, 1956).

SU̧ (ISUWU)
Where spoken: B.C., on the extreme south coast of Bimbia promontory (Ardener).
Number: Under 500 (NBi); 140 (Ardener).
These four units 'form for practical purposes a clear sub-group' though 'Isuwu is perhaps somewhat more distinctive' (Ardener).

DU̧ALA
Where spoken: C., around Douala estuary.
Number: 22,927 (Ardener).
DUALA is used as a commercial language and medium of communication over a wide area in the western part of Cameroun and the southern part of B.C.; it is also used by missions. According to Ardener, however, it is now being superseded by Pidgin as a lingua franca.

KƆLƐ
Where spoken: B.C., in small settlements on the coast north-west of the MBOKO (Ardener).
Number: 307 (Ardener).

BO̧DI̧MAN
Where spoken: C., on both banks of R. Wouri south of Yabassi.
Number: 2,006 (IESC).
Described in NBi as 'a dialect of DUALA closely related to PO̧ŊGO̧ and O̧LI̧', but not investigated by the NBBS team. See also under O̧LI̧ below.

O̧LI̧
Where spoken: C., Rég. Moungo, S.-D. Yabassi, on both banks of R. Wouri just above the estuary.
Number: 3,621 (IESC).
There are two branches of the tribe, WURI BƆSWA and WURI BWILI, said by informants to speak the same language (NBi). According to MG2 this is the language spoken by the BO̧DI̧MAN (see above).

PO̧NGO̧
Where spoken: C., Rég. Moungo, in the southern part of S.-D. Mbanga on both sides of the road to Bonabéri, and westwards to the B.C. border.
Number: 6,584 (IESC).
Spoken by old people (the younger people in the tribe having adopted DU̧ALA, with which it is inter-intelligible) (NBi).

MU̧NGO̧
Where spoken: C., Rég. Moungo, and B.C., Victoria Div., in scattered villages on both banks of R. Moungo around Tiko and down to the coast.
Number: B.C., estimated at not more than 1,000 (NBi).
There are 'slight differences... between the varieties of this language spoken on British and French banks of the Mungo' (NBi). It is closely related to PO̧NGO̧; the two are considered as one unit in MG2.

MỤLỊMBA

Where spoken: C., in scattered settlements along the coast on both sides of the mouth of R. Sanaga.

Number: 3,692 (IESC).

†BALƆD—see MBO Group, p. 3.

†BƆNKĘD—see MBO Group.

'S. BAKOKO'. According to NBi Johnston's 'S. BAKOKO' is 'far removed from MBƐNƐ [BASA Group] and more closely related to DỤALA'. In NBi it is stated that Guthrie agrees with this view. But see BAKƆGƆ (A.43b) under BASA Group.

†'N. BAKOKO'

Where spoken: C., Rég. Moungo, in the extreme south-east of S.-D. Mbanga.

'A language which, while its vocabulary relates it closely to N. MBƐNƐ [BASA Group], shows unmistakable signs of being grammatically a mixture of DỤALA and BULU type languages' (NBi).

BUBE GROUP

Where spoken: C., Fernando Po, Rio Muni.

MG3		Ardener[1]	Other names
BUBE	A.31/o		Bubi, Ediya, Fernandian
BATANGA	A.32/*:	TANGA	
⎧ BANƆƆ	A.32a	NƆƆ	Banaka, Banoh, Noho, Noko
⎩ BAPOKO	A.32b	POKO	Naka, Puku
⎧ YASA	A.33a/o	YASA	
⎩ KOMBE	A.33b/o		Ngumbi
BENGA	A.34/*		

BUBE

Where spoken: On the island of Fernando Po.

According to MG2 there are several dialects (not named), on which there is little reliable information.

BATANGA

This would appear to be a geographical name, covering two dialects:

BANƆƆ

Where spoken: C., on the coast near Kribi.
Number: c. 2,000 (MG2).

BAPOKO

Where spoken: C., on the coast near Grand Batanga.
Number: A very small group (MG2).

YASA and KOMBE

Where spoken: C. and Rio Muni, scattered along the coast.
Number: Few (MG2).

BENGA

Where spoken: Rio Muni, along the southern coast; also in Gabon, and on the island of Corisco.
Number: Small groups (MG2).

[1] Op. cit.

(10)

BASA GROUP

Where spoken: B.C., C.

MG3		NBi		Other names
†(BALOŊ	A.13/*)	BALOŊ	21a	
See MBO Group, p. 3.				
†(BƆNKEŊ	A.14/*)	BƆŊKEŊ	21b	
See MBO Group.				
LƆMBĮ	A.41/o	LƆMBĮ	21c	Barombi, Rombi
BANKǪN	A.42/*	BAŊKǪN	21d	Abo
		†'N. BAKOKO'	21e	
See DUALA Group, p. 6.				
BASA	A.43:	N. MBƐNƐ:		Bassa, Koko, Mvele
⎧ MBƐNƐ	A.43a/*			
⎪		⎧ NDOKBELE	21f	
⎪		⎪ YABASI	21g	
⎪		⎪ NDOKPENDA	21h	
⎨		⎪ NYAMTAM	21i	Nyamtan
⎪		⎨ DIBENG	21j	
⎪		⎪ NDOKAMA	21k	
⎪		⎪ BAKEM	21l	
⎪		⎪ MBAŊG	21m	
⎪		⎩ DĮBŲM	21n	
		(d̑įbųm)		
⎩ BAKƆGƆ	A.43b/*	(S. BAKOKO')		
BANƐN	A.44/*	BANƐN:	22a:	Banend, Penin, Penyin
		⎧ NDOKBIAKAT	22a.i	
		⎪ NDOKTUNA	22a.ii	
		⎪ NDOGBANG	22a.iii	
		⎨ NDOGBANOL	22a.iv	
		⎪ LOGANANGA	22a.v	
		⎪ ELING	22a.vi	
		⎩ ITUNDU	22a.vii	
		BƆNƐK	22b	Ponek
		((ɔtaŋg)atɔmb)		
MANDĮ	A.46/*	MANDĮ	22c	Lemande
		YAMBETA	22e	
NYƆ̃'Ɔ̃	A.45/*	⎧ NYƆ̃'Ɔ̃	22d	Nyokon
		⎩ FUŊ		

In MG2 the BASA Group includes BANƐN, &c.; in NBi there are two separate Groups, N. MBƐNƐ (BASA) and BANƐN ('a close relationship exists between NYƆ̃'Ɔ̃, BƆNƐK, MANDĮ, and BANƐN'), but the boundaries of the two Groups 'merge to such an extent that it is hard to say which dialects should be attributed to MBƐNƐ and which to BANƐN' (NBii).

BASA GROUP

†BALOŊ—see MBO Group, p. 3.

†BƆNKEŊ—see MBO Group.

LƆMBĮ

Where spoken: B.C., Kumba Div., in two enclaves round the Barombi crater lakes, and one west of Kumba on both banks of the upper Makunge river.
Number: 1,046 (Talbot).
LƆMBĮ is very closely related to BANKǪN, and the 'BAROMBI' are traditionally descended from the BANKǪN (NBi).

BANKǪN

Where spoken: C., Rég. Moungo, in the northern part of S.-D. Mbanga, between R. Moungo and the eastern border of the S.-D., i.e. almost to R. Wouri between 4° 10' and 4° 30' N.
Number: 10,232 (IESC).
There are reported to be two different peoples, ABO and BANKON, in this area, but informants state that there is only one language (NBi).

†'N. BAKOKO'—see DUALA Group, p. 6.

BASA. This name is used in MG3 to cover two main dialects. Further subdivisions of MBƐNƐ are made in NBi.

MBƐNƐ

Where spoken: C., in a large area to the north-east and east of Douala.
Number: c. 150,000 (MG2).
There are many small dialects of the MBƐNƐ Cluster, most of which were not investigated by the NBBS team; many of the names listed in NBi are administrative names of tribes, clans, or areas. The following dialects are dealt with in NBi:

YABASI (a place-name), in Rég. Moungo, in the northern part of S.-D. Yabassi.
MBAŊG, in the northern and north-western parts of S.-D. Yabassi.
DĮBŲM, in Rég. Bamiléke and Rég. Moungo, in the south of S.-D. Bafang and the north of S.-D. Yabassi.
Number: 6,000 (IESC).
MBAŊG and DĮBŲM are almost identical, and YABASI very closely related. There is some vocabulary relationship with 'N. BAKOKO'.

BAKƆGƆ

Where spoken: C., just in from the coast to the north and south of Douala (MG2).
Number: c. 20,000 (MG2).

BANƐN

Where spoken: C. The BANƐN area as a whole stretches approximately from just east of Yabassi to east of Ndikiniméki in a narrow belt.

BASA GROUP

Number: 'BANEN proper' 24,426 (IESC)+*c.* 2,000 in Douala.[1]

BANƐN consists of a large number of dialects, most of which were not investigated by the NBBS team; many of the names listed in NBi are administrative names of tribes, clans, or areas. The following dialects are dealt with in NBi:

BONƐK, at Bonek village on the Ndikiniméki–Bafia road, just within the limits of S.-D. Bafia.

Number: under 50.

Spoken only by the village elders, the younger people now speaking 'BANƐN'.

MANDỊ, north-west of Bafia.
Number: 1,984 (IESC); 2,543 (Dugast).[2]

YAMBETA, east of the main BANƐN area.
Number: 1,984 (IESC), 2,543 (Dugast).[3]

MG2 classes MANDỊ as a separate unit from BANƐN, and says that 'the people known as Yambeta and Bonek also speak this language'.

A 'standard' form of BANƐN is used by missions and administrators, and has become the lingua franca of a large part of the area.

NYƆ'Ɔ

Where spoken: C., Rég. Mbam, north-west of S.-D. Ndikiniméki; Rég. Moungo west of S.-D. Yabassi.

Number: 3,900 (IESC); 3,002 (Dugast).[4]

A dialect called FUD is spoken at Kinding (NBi).

---

[1] Dugast, 'The Banen, Bafia and Balom of the French Cameroons'. In: *Peoples of the Central Cameroons* (Eth. Survey, 1954).
[2] Ibid.
[3] Ibid.
[4] Ibid.

BAFIA GROUP

Where spoken: C.

MG3		NBi		Other names
FA' (lə-)	A.51/*	FA'	23	Fak, Balom
KAALOŊ (lə-) or MBƆŊ	A.52/*	KAALOŊ	25	
KPA (ɾə-)	A.53/*	KPA (ɾə-)	24	Bafia
ŊGAYABA (lə-)	A.54/*	ŊGAYABA (lə-)	26	Djanti

The 'SANAGA' Group (see below) is included in this Group in NBi.

FA' (lə-)

Where spoken: On both banks of R. Mbam at its confluence with R. Noun.
Number: 3,846 (IESC).

KAALOŊ or MBƆŊ (lə-)

Where spoken: On the right bank of R. Mbam beyond the Noun confluence.
Number: c. 50.

KPA (ɾə-) (BAFIA)

Where spoken: Rég. Mbam, S.-D. Bafia, in Bafia town and the immediate surroundings.
Number: 12,093 (IESC); 17,257 (Dugast).[1]
Dugast names three subdivisions of the tribe: BEKPA, BEKKE, and BAPE.

ŊGAYABA (lə-)

Where spoken: S.-D. Bafia, in seven villages on the eastern slopes of the Djanti and Niabidi mountains.
Number: Under 1,000 (IESC).

[1] Op. cit.

'SANAGA' GROUP

Where spoken: C.

MG3		NBi		Other names
NGƆRƆ	A.61/*	ŊGƆRƆ	27a	
YAMBASA	A.62/*	YAMBASA	29	
		'SANAGA'	30:	
MANGĮSA	A.63/*	⎧ MAŊGĮSA	30a	
BACƐNGA	A.64/*	⎩ BƐTSIŊGA	30b	Betzinga
		CĮDGA (tʃiŋga)	28	Bundum, Kombe
BATĮ	A.65/0	BATĮ	27b	

This Group is considered as distinct from the BAFIA Group (see p. 13) in MG2. 'In many respects this group is one on its own and does not display much relationship with the previous ones. Although it is difficult to demonstrate, nevertheless there is much about these languages which seems to suggest that they represent a mingling of two distinct sources, one of which appears to have affinities with Bantu languages right outside the area.' On the other hand, 'the general "feel" of the material to hand causes us to mention in the same breath such languages as [the BAFIA and "SANAGA" Groups]'. In NBi the term 'SANAGA' is used in a more restricted sense, to cover the speech of 'numerous heterogeneous sub-tribes who employ roughly the same language'.

Tessmann's BATI-MBAM appears to correspond to this Group.[1]

NGƆRƆ

Where spoken: S.-D. Bafia, on the left bank of R. Mbam in the valley of its affluent R. Ngoro, in eight villages.

Almost identical with Johnston's BA-TI (BACƐŊGA).

YAMBASA

Where spoken: South of Bafia on the west side of R. Mbam and R. Sanaga.
Number: 26,721 (Dugast).[2]

Dugast quotes L. K. Anderson as stating that YAMBASA is related to BULU (see YAUNDE-FANG Group, p. 18), and shows 'clear signs of non-Bantu influence'.

MANGĮSA

Where spoken: In the bend of R. Sanaga above the Mbam confluence.
Number: c. 14,000 (MG2).

There appears to be some confusion between BƐTSIŊGA and CĮDGA, which, according to NBi, 'should not be confused'. No locality is given for BƐTSIŊGA (one of the 'SANAGA' dialects) in NBi, and that given for BACƐNGA in MG2 more or less coincides with that given for CĮDGA in NBi.

[1] *Die Völker und Sprachen Kameruns.*   [2] Op. cit.

'SANAGA' GROUP

BACƐNGA (BƐTSIDGA)

Where spoken: On the north side of R. Sanaga above the Mbam confluence (MG2).
Number: c. 10,000 (MG2).

CĮDGA

Where spoken: On both banks of R. Mbam just above its confluence with R. Sanaga east of Bafia town. 'This is the location of the informant's village and immediate vicinity' (NBi).
Number: (CĮDGA and BƐTSIDGA together) 15,562 (Dugast).[1]

BATĮ

Where spoken: Along the west bank of R. Lihoua, near its confluence with R. Sanaga.
Number: 'A small group' (MG2).

Dugast, Johnston, and Tessmann include CĮDGA under BATĮ, which is described as extending to various localities between 11° 30'–12° E. and 3° 30'–4° 30' N.

---

[1] Op. cit.

YAUNDE-FANG GROUP

Where spoken: C., also Rio Muni and G.

MG3		NBi		Other names
ETON	A.71/*			
EWONDO:				
⎧EWONDO	A.72a/o			Jaunde, Yaunde
⎪MVËLË	A.72b/*	YƐZŲM (MVËLË)[1]	31	Yesoum, Yezum
		⎧⎧AVƏK	32	Bafök, Bafuk, Bavek
		⎨⎨LEPƏK	32a	
		⎪⎪? MƐDGAD		
		⎩⎩YAṢEM	32b	
⎪YANGAFËK	A.72d/*	YADGAFUK[1]	33	
⎩BAKJA[2]	A.72c/*			Badjia
⎰BËBËLË	A.73/*	BËBËLË	35	Bamvele
⎱GBÏGBÏL	A.73/o	GBÏGBÏL	34	Bobili(s)
		EKĮ	36	Badjia, Mvang, Omvang
⎰BŲLŲ	A.74/*			Boulou, Bulu
⎱BËNË				Bane
		†('N. BAKOKO'	21c)	

See DUALA Group, p. 6.

FAD	A.75/*:			Fãn, Fañwe, Pahouin,
⎰NTUM				Pamue, Pangwe, &c.
⎱MAKE				

In NBi, only those languages or dialects have been dealt with which are located on or near the northern Bantu borderline. 'In such an area, where relationships are so close, where language names are so numerous, varied and bogus, and tribal history and geography so chequered, it is doubtful whether any complete and incontestably correct demographic statement will ever be made. . . . A strange feature of this area is the unreliability of statements on intercomprehension of languages or dialects' (NBi).

ETON

Where spoken: C., in a thickly populated area to the north-west of Yaounde.
Number: 111,738 (IESC).

EWONDO (YAUNDE)

Where spoken: C., south-west of Yaounde in the direction of Lolodorf and the coast.
Number: 93,027 (IESC).

The most westerly group of EWONDO-speakers is known as EVUZOK (MG2).

'EWONDO populaire' is used as a medium of intercourse throughout the central part of Cameroun, extending as far as Yoko, by Africans whose mother tongue is related to the Group, by missionaries and in administration.

[1] In this Group there is a very central vowel represented in MG3 by Ë and in NBi by Ë or ə.
[2] **bak-** (closed syllable)+**-ja** (MG., personal communication).

MVËLË (YƐZŲM)

Where spoken: C., east of Yaounde, in the direction of Akonolinga and Nanga Eboko (MG2). In NBi the term YƐZŲM is used in a more restricted sense, and the locality is given as the extreme south-west corner of S.-D. Nanga Eboko, Rég. Nyong et Sanaga, between 11°–12° 30′ E. and 4° 11′–4° 30′ N.

Number: Nearly 140,000, in many different sub-tribes (MG2); 8,075 (IESC)—i.e. presumably 'YƐZŲM proper'.

In MG2 OMVAD is named as one of the MVËLË-speaking sub-tribes (but see EKĮ below).

'The YƐZŲM are said to understand the YEKABA, BŲLŲ, and EWONDO' (NBi).

The following dialects are listed separately in NBi, with the comment 'The similarity of AVƏK vocabulary [to YƐZŲM] is too great for inter-intelligibility not to exist between these two dialects'.

AVƏK, LEPƏK, MƐDGAD (?), YAȘƐM

Where spoken: Rég. Nyong et Sanaga, S.-D. Nanga Eboko, in three small enclaves north-east of Nanga Eboko; Rég. Mbam, S.-D. Yoko, north of Yoko at Lena (50 km.); south-east of Yoko at Mengang (10 km.) and Medjamboum (20 km.); west-south-west of Yoko at Yassem (100 km.); at Issandja in the Bafia area 120 km. south of Yoko on the main road.

Number: 5,352 (IESC), including speakers of YANGAFËK.

YANGAFËK

Where spoken: S.-D. Nanga Eboko, west of Nanga Eboko on the right bank of R. Sanaga; Rég. Mbam, east of Bafia on the road to Yoko.

Number: see under AVƏK, &c.

AVƏK, &c. and YANGAFËK appear to be almost identical, but informants 'would not admit to intercomprehension' (NBi). BAFÖK (i.e. AVƏK) is included under YANGAFËK in MG2.

BAKJA

Where spoken: South-east of Nanga Eboko.
Number: c. 14,000 (MG2).

The YEKABA are included among BAKJA-speakers in MG2; according to NBi BADJIA is one of the names of EKĮ (see below).

BËBËLË

Where spoken: East of Nanga Eboko.
Number: c. 18,000 (MG2).

GBÏGBÏL

Where spoken: Rég. Lom et Kadeï, S.-D. Bertoua, north-west of Bertoua in the area enclosed by R. Sanaga, R. Sesse, R. Long, and R. Do.
Number: 6,247 (IESC).

There is close vocabulary resemblance to YANGAFËK, and 'remarkable intercomprehension exists with the BAMVËLË' (NBi).

EKI

Where spoken: S.-D. Nanga Eboko, also perhaps S.-D. Doumé.
Number: c. 2,900 (NBi, from local administration figures).

'As regards the names given to languages spoken by the MVANG, it is pointless to argue which is the more correct, since the various branches of this tribe no longer speak the same language' (NBi). EKI is spoken in two villages in S.-D. Nanga Eboko (Biwong and Mimbele); numerous sub-chefferies or clans in the S.-D. are said to speak the same language. These include YEBANDA, YENGONG, YEMBANI, and YETCHOA. The MVANG MAKONA in S.-D. Doumé are said to be losing their language in favour of MÄKAA (see p. 19) and the MVANG of S.-D. Akonolinga are said now to speak MAKE (see under FAṆ below).

BULU

Where spoken: Over a vast area in the southern part of Cameroun between 10° and 13° E.
Number: c. 110,000 (MG2).

BULU sub-tribes named in MG2 are: YENGONO, YEMBAMA, YELINDA, ZAMAN.

BULU is used by American Protestant missions and in administration, and is a medium of intercourse as far north as Bertoua.

BĖNĖ

Where spoken: North of the BULU area towards Mbalmayo and Yaounde.
Number: c. 60,000 (MG2).

†'N. BAKOKO'—see DUALA Group, p. 6.

FAṆ

Where spoken: Over a vast area in the southern part of Cameroun and in Rio Muni and Gabon.
Number: probably c. 200,000 (MG2).

The northern variety of this language is sometimes known as NTUM, the southern as MAKE.

The British and Foreign Bible Society's list distinguishes between:
    FANG of Gabon (parts of the Bible), and
    FANG of Ogowe (PAHOUIN) (the whole Bible).

MAKAA GROUP

Where spoken: C., extending into O.-C., also G. and M.-C.

MG3		NBi		*Other names*
MVUMBO	A.81/*			Ngumba
SO	A.82/*			
MAKAA	A.83/*	MÄKAA	38	Maka
NJĚM	A.84/*	NDJĚM	39	Djem, Dzimu, Kozime, Zimu
BAJUE				Badjue
KONABEM	A.85/*	KONABEMB	43	Konabembe
BƐKWIL				Bakwele
MBIMU	A.86:			
MƐDJIMƐ	A.86a/*	MƐDJIMƐ (mɛdime)	40a	Medzime
		BAAGƎTO (ɓaayəto)	40b	N. Bangantu
MPÕMPÕ	A.86b/*			Bombo, Boumboum, Mbumbum, Mpompo, Kaka of Sala
MPIƐMƆ	A.86c/*	MPIƐMƆ BIDJUKI	41	Mbimu
BOMWALI	A.87/*			

† ? BƐTHƐN (see also KAKA Group, p. 22).

'A most loosely knit and unbalanced conglomeration of languages' (NBi).

MVUMBO

Where spoken: In several distinct areas in the west of Cameroun and in the north-west corner of Rio Muni (MG2).
Number: c. 10,000 (MG2).
The most southerly speakers are known as MABI (MABEA) or BISIWO.

SO

Where spoken: C., S.-D. Akonolinga.
Number: c. 6,000 (MG2).

MAKAA

Where spoken: C., S.-D.'s Bertoua, Doumé, Abong-Mbang, Mbalmayo, Akonolinga, Sangmelima, &c., in an irregular-shaped area with main centre 12° 30'–13° 35' E., 3° 50'–4° 35' N.; enclaves at 13° 35' E., 4° 45' N. and 12° 35' E., 4° 15' N.; other scattered enclaves between 12°–12° 25' E. and 3° 20'–3° 45' N. (NBi, mainly from IESC).
Number: 51,633 (IESC).
There are many divergent dialects.

MAKAA GROUP

NJĚM

Where spoken: C., scattered in a vast area of otherwise uninhabited forest south of the MAKAA.
Number: c. 20,000 (MG2).
Speakers of NJĚM include the peoples known as DZIMU, BADJUE, and ESEL.
NJĚM is used as a medium of intercourse by Africans speaking related languages in the eastern part of C. and in western O.-C. These people are collectively known as KOZIME (NBi).

KǪNABẸM

Where spoken: C., south of Yokadouma.
Number: c. 3,000 (MG2).
Also spoken by the BOMAN (MG2).

BƐKWỊL

Where spoken: M.-C., in Souanké and Sembe districts; G., in Mékambo district.
Number: c. 5,000 (MG2).

MƐDJỊMƐ

Where spoken: C., Rég. Lom et Kadeï, on the right bank of R. Doumé, west of R. Mbang.
Number: 2,684 (IESC).

BAAGƏTO (N. BANGANTU)[1]

Where spoken: C., Rég. Lom et Kadeï, in the valley of R. Doumé above its confluence with R. Kadeï.
Number: 1,711 (IESC).
MƐDJỊMƐ and BAAGƏTO are two names for the same language, spoken by two different peoples, according to both NBi and MG2. It is said to be easily understood by speakers of MPỊƐMƆ, KǪNABẸM, &c. (NBi).

MBIMU. This is the name used in MG3 for a Dialect Cluster which includes MƐDJỊMƐ and also the following two dialects:

MPƆ̃MPƆ̃

Where spoken: C., just to the west of Yokadouma.
Number: c. 4,000 (MG2).
This is the 'KAKA of Sala' of Ouzilleau.[2]

MPỊƐMƆ

Where spoken: On the C.-O.-C. border east of Yokadouma.
Number: MPỊƐMƆ 3,977, BỊDJỤKỊ 3,419 (IESC).
The MPỊƐMƆ and BỊDJỤKỊ speak the same language, the 'MPỊƐMƆ proper'

---

[1] To be distinguished from 'S. BANGANTU' or BADGANDO, a non-Bantu language (see NBi, p. 58), also from DGANDǪ (see NGANDO Group, p. 33).
[2] 'Notes sur les Pygmées de la Sanga' (*Rev. Ethnogr. et Sociol.*, 1911).

MAKAA GROUP

being north of Yokadouma on the road to Batouri, the BIDJUKI in Rég. Lom et Kadeï, S.-D. Yokadouma, and in O.-C., Rég. Haute-Sangha, D. Nola, along the Yokadouma–Nola track (NBi).

Other 'clans' of the MPIƐMƆ tribe (for which no population figures are given) are BIAKUMBO, BIKUM, and KPABILI.

BỌMWALỊ

Where spoken: M.-C., mainly on the south bank of R. Ngoko and R. Sangha for about 120 miles downstream from Soufflay.

The people in the eastern part of this area are known as LINO.

†BƐTHƐN is said to be a transition language between AZƆM (see note under KWAKUM, p. 22) and MAKAA, and to be spoken in villages in the PỌL area, but nothing is known of it (NBi).

There is some similarity between this Language Group and the KAKA Group (see p. 22).

KAKA GROUP

Where spoken: C., O.-C.

MG3		NBi		Other names
KWAKUM	A.91/*	KWAKUM	48	Akpwakum, Bakum, Pakum
		? AZƆM		
{POL	A.92/*	POL (poli)	46	Pul
{PƆMƆ		PƆMƆ	47	
KAKƆ	A.93/*	KAKƆ	45	Kaka, Yaka
		†BƐTHƐN (see also MAKAA Group, p. 19).		

KWAKUM

Where spoken: C., mainly in S.-D. Doumé.
Number: A few thousand (MG2).
AZƆM is said to be spoken in the POL area in S.-D. Bertoua. Nothing is known of it, but it may be a KWAKUM dialect, as some maps show a KWAKUM enclave in this area (NBi).

POL

Where spoken: C. (*a*) S.-D. Bertoua, north of the Bertoua–Deng Deng track in three villages; (*b*) S.-D. Doumé, on the right bank of R. Doumé east of Doumé town, in the villages of Grand Pol and Petit Pol; (*c*) S.-D. Batouri, 7 miles south of Batouri in Kombo village.
Number: 2,200 (IESC), probably including speakers of AZƆM.

PƆMƆ

Where spoken: O.-C., in a few scattered villages along the east bank of R. Sangha for about 60 miles below Bayanga.
POL and PƆMƆ are very closely related.

KAKƆ

Where spoken: C., Rég. Lom et Kadeï, S.-D. Batouri; O.-C., Rég. Haute-Sangha, D. Berbérati, about 13° 40′–15° 30′ E., 4°–4° 35′ N.
Number: C. 36,932 (IESC).
The material for this area given by Strümpell[1] is almost identical with KAKƆ as recorded by the NBBS team at Batouri. The KAKƆ south-west of Ngaoundéré no longer speak their own language, owing to intermarriage with the MBUM (non-Bantu-speaking). Nothing further is known of the KAKƆ enclaves among the non-Bantu GBAYA of Bertoua referred to by Dugast (cited in NBi).

There is some similarity between this Group and the MAKAA Group (see p. 19).

†BƐTHƐN is said to be a transition language between AZƆM and MAKAA.

---

[1] 'Wörterverzeichnis der Heidensprachen Adamauas' (*Z. Ethnol.*, 1910).

MYENE SINGLE UNIT

Where spoken: G.

MG3		*Other names*
MYƐNƐ:	B.11:	
⎧ MPONGWĘ	B.11a/*	Mpongoué, Npongué, Pongoué
⎪ RONGO	B.11b/*	Orungu
⎨ GALWA	B.11c/*	Galoa, Omyene
⎪ DYŲMBA	B.11d/*	Adjumba, Adyumba
⎩ NKƆMĮ	B.11e/*	Nkomi
		ENENGA (Walker)[1]

According to former statements these dialects must have had a considerable importance in the past; they now appear to be rapidly becoming extinct (MG2).

MPONGWĘ

Where spoken: On both sides of the Gabon estuary.
Number: c. 1,000.[2]

RONGO

Where spoken: In the Cap Lopez area on the coast.
Number: Nearly 2,000.

GALWA

Where spoken: Near Lambaréné and round L. Onangué.
Number: c. 2,000.

DYŲMBA

Where spoken: On the north bank of R. Ogooué near Lambaréné.
Number: 'A small group.'

NKƆMĮ

Where spoken: Along the coast north of Setté Cama.
Number: c. 5,000.

Walker adds ENENGA to this Cluster.

'Union OMYENE' has been used for Bible translation.

---

[1] 'Les Idiomes gabonais. Similarités et divergences' (*Bull. Inst. Ét. Centrafr.*, 1955).
[2] Figures for this Group from MG2.

KOTA GROUP[1]

Where spoken: G., M.-C.

MG3		Other names
SƐKIYANI	B.21/*	Bulu, Sheke
KƐLƐ	B.22:	
⎧ W. KƐLƐ (dį-)	B.22a/*	
⎨ NGƆM (a-)	B.22b/*	Bangomo
⎩ BỤBĮ	B.22c/o	
MBADWƐ	B.23/o	
WỤMBVỤ	B.24/*	
KỌTA (i-)	B.25/*	Mahongwe, Shake

SƐKIYANI
Where spoken: G., on the coast north of Libreville.
Number: Almost extinct.[2]

KƐLƐ (dį-)
Where spoken: G., on the Gabon estuary.
Number: A very small group.

NGƆM (a-)
Where spoken: G. (*a*) on the north bank of R. Ogooué between N'Djolé and Booué; (*b*) east of Sindara; (*c*) in region of Koulamotou; (*d*) in the neighbourhood of Mékambo far to the north-east.
Number: c. 11,000.
According to DB closely allied to DỤMA (see NJABI Group, p. 27).

BỤBĮ
Where spoken: G., west of Koulamotou.
Number: c. 4,000.

MBADWƐ
Where spoken: M.-C., west of Franceville.
Number: c. 2,000.

WỤMBVỤ
Where spoken: G., east of Ndendé.
Number: c. 4,000.

KỌTA (i-)[3]
Where spoken: G. and M.-C., mainly in a region bounded by R. Livindo and upper Ogooué river, also scattered in M.-C. in groups as far separated as just south of Ouesso, and in the region of Ombaïa and Sibiti.
Number: c. 28,000.

[1] Called KELE Group in MG3. The name KOTA, that of the language spoken by the largest number of people, is used here to avoid confusion with the better-known KELE (LOKELE) (see p. 46).
[2] Figures for this Group from MG2.
[3] To be distinguished from KOTA in the NGANDO Group (p. 33).

TSOGO GROUP?

Where spoken: G.

	MG3		Other names
	TSƆGƆ (ɣę-)	B.31/*	Mitsogo, Apindji
	KANDE	B.32/o	Okande

TSƆGƆ (ɣę-)
  Where spoken: North-east of Mouila for about 50 miles from R. N'Gougnié.

KANDE
  Where spoken: Near Booué.
  Number: Almost extinct.
  The only information available is non-linguistic.[1]

[1] MG, personal communication.

SHIRA-PUNU GROUP

Where spoken: G., extending into M.-C.

MG3		Other names
SIRA (i-)	B.41/*	Shira
SANGU (yi-)	B.42/*	Shango
PUNU (yi-)	B.43/*	
LUMBU (i-)	B.44/*	

SIRA (i-)

Where spoken: G., for about 50 miles to the south-west of R. N'Gougnié, between Fougamou and Mouila.
Number: c. 17,000.[1]

SANGU (yi-)

Where spoken: G., in a narrow belt north-east and south-west of Mimongo.
Number: c. 18,000.

PUNU (yi-)

Where spoken: Over a large area on both sides of the G.–M.-C. border, just inland from the coastal plain.
Number: c. 46,000.

LUMBU (i-)

Where spoken: On both sides of the G.–M.-C. border, on the coastal plain.
Number: c. 12,000.

These languages show a close relationship to the NJABI Group (see p. 27).

[1] Figures for this Group from MG2.

NJABI GROUP

Where spoken: G., M.-C.

MG3		Other names
DỤMA (lį-dʼụma)	B.51/0	Adouma, Aduma, Douma, Duma
		WANDJI
TSAANGI (i-)	B.52/*	Tsangi, Tcengui, Tchangui
NZƐBỊ (yį-nzɛɓį)	B.53/*	Bandzabi, Ndjabi, Ndjevi
		VILI

Adam[1] includes these languages in the TEKE Group, as well as those in the MBETE Group (p. 28). In MG2 attention is directed to the relationship between these Groups. MG now states, however, that his original grouping has been confirmed by his recent researches.[2] Some additional names given by Adam are added here.

DỤMA (lį-)

Where spoken: G., on the left bank of R. Ogooué above and below Lastourville (Adam).
Number: c. 10,000 (MG2), 2,000 (Adam).

WANDJI

Where spoken: G., D. Franceville at Mwanda and in the southern part of D. Lastourville.
Number: 6,000 (Adam).

TSAANGI (i-)

Where spoken: On both sides of the G.-M.-C. border around and to the west of Mossendjo.
Number: 10,000 (MG2).

NZƐBỊ (yį-)

Where spoken: On both sides of the border over a large area astride 2° S.
Number: 20,000 (MG2), 40,000 in G. (Adam).

VILI

Where spoken: In a few villages on R. N'Gougnié (Adam).

---

[1] 'Dialectes du Gabon: la famille Téké' (*Bull. Inst. Ét. Centrafr.*, 1954).
[2] Personal communication, 1957.

MBETE GROUP

Where spoken: G., M.-C.

MG, 1957[1]		Other names
MBETE	B.61/*	Mbede, Obamba
MBAAMA (yi-)	B.62/*	Mbamba, Bakota[2]
MINDUUMO	B.63/*	Ndumu, Doumbou, Ondoumbo

MBETE

Where spoken: M.-C., Districts Kélé and Ewo (Eouo), also in Districts Zanaga and Sibiti; G., Districts Okundja, Franceville, and Lastourville (Adam).[3]

Number: M.-C. 35,000, G. 20,000 (probably including MBAMBA) (Adam).

MBAAMA (yi-)

Where spoken: North-east of Franceville.
Number: c. 12,000 (MG2).

MINDUUMO

Where spoken: In the immediate neighbourhood of Franceville (MG2); also on R. Passa, and on R. Ogooué towards Lastourville (Adam).

Number: c. 4,000 (MG2).

Adam gives the names of several dialects:
KUYA, EPIGI, KAÑANDJOHO, NYAÑI.

---

[1] Personal communication; amended spelling of names.
[2] The use of the name ba-KOTA for the ba-MBAAMA by their neighbours has led in the past to confusion with the ba-KOTA proper (p. 24).
[3] Op. cit.

TEKE-YANS GROUP

Where spoken: G., M.-C., C.B.

MG, 1957[1]		Other names
N. TEGE	B.71/*:	Teke
⎰ TEGE (ka-)		Tégué
⎱ NJINIDI (ka-)		Ndjinini, Njikini, Nzikini,[2] Djikini
NGUNGWEL	B.72/*	Ngungulu, Ngungwoni, Mpŭ, Mpŭmpŭ,[3] Ngangoulou
⎧ BOÕ (e-)	B.73/*	Boma
⎪ NJINJU		Ndzindzihu, Nziku, Nzinzihu, Ndzikou
⎨ WUÕ		
⎩ KWE		
KUKWA	B.73/*	Cikuya, Kukuya, Koukouya
DEE (esi-)	B.74/*	
BALI	B.75/*	Ambali, Tio, Teo, Tyo
WUUMU (i-)	B.76/*	Wumu
S. W. TEGE	B.77/*:	Teke
⎧ TSAAYI		Tsayi, Ntsaayi, Tsaye
⎨ LAALI (i-)		Lali
⎩ YAA (i-)		Yaka
FUMU		Ifumu, Mfumu
TIINI (ki-)	B.81/*	Tende, Tiene
BOMA (ki-)	B.82/*	Buma
MFINU (e-)	B.83/*	Funika, Mfununga[4]
YANS (j-):	B.85/*	Yansi, Yanzi
⎧ DĬ, DID, DZID	B.87/*	Dzing, Idzing
⎨ MBUUN	B.88/*	Mbunu, Mbunda
⎩ YEEI	B.88/*	Yey
and many other dialects.		

This Group is composed of Groups B.70 and B.80 of MG3, with some omissions. Spelling of some of the names is amended in the light of new researches, as is the grouping of dialects into Clusters. Apparent discrepancy in the rendering of vowels is due to the presence of five-vowel, seven-vowel, and multivowel languages in the same Group.

For DJIA and SAKATA (B.84) see MONGO-NKUNDO Group, p. 48.

For NGUL (B.86) see p. 32.

TEGE (ka-) and NJINIDI (ka-) (perhaps two names for the same language, with slight variants).

Where spoken: M.-C., TEGE in the neighbourhood of Eouo, NJINIDI on R. Alima in the region of Okoyo.

Number: TEGE 15,000, NJINIDI 9,000 (Adam).[5]

[1] Personal communication. [2] NJIKINI is the name used by the MBAAMA.
[3] The name MPŬ used in MG2 is that of a NGUNGWEL clan.
[4] Names used by the ba-KONGO. [5] Op. cit.

NGUNGWEL

Where spoken: M.-C., north of Gamboma.

BOÕ

Where spoken: M.-C., on the plateau west of M'Pouya.
Number: 6,000 (Adam).

NJINJU

Where spoken: Around Djambala.
Number: 9,000 (Adam).

WUÕ and KWE

Where spoken: In much the same area as the above.

KUKWA

Where spoken: M.-C., on the plateau in the neighbourhood of Djambala.
Number: 11,000 (Adam).

ŊEE (esi-)

Where spoken: C.B., inland from R. Congo north of R. Kwa.

BALI

Where spoken: M.-C. and C.B., on both sides of Stanley Pool.
Number: 'A small group' (MG3).

WUUMU (i-)

Where spoken: C.B., south of Léopoldville.
Number: 'A small group' (MG3).

TSAAYI

Where spoken: M.-C., in a narrow belt north-west of Zanaga.
Number: c. 30,000 (Adam).

LAALI (i-)

Where spoken: M.-C. (*a*) east of Sibiti; (*b*) north of Sibiti.

YAA (i-)

Where spoken: M.-C., in the region of Sibiti.
Number: c. 2,000.

FUMU (i-)

Where spoken: Around Franceville.
Number: c. 200 (MG, 1957).
This language was believed to be extinct, but speakers of it were discovered in 1957.

TI̧INI (ki-)

Where spoken: C.B., inland from Bolobo on R. Congo.
Number: 15,000.

BOMA (ki-)

Where spoken: C.B., inland from Mushie on the north bank of R. Fimi and R. Kwa, and on the opposite bank of R. Kwa.
Number: 8,000.

MFINU (e-)

Where spoken: C.B., north of R. Fimi, west of L. Léopold II.

YANS (i̧-)

Where spoken: C.B., south of R. Kasaï near its confluence with R. Kamtsha to below Banningville.
There are many dialects of YANS, including:
  DĬ, DIŊ, or DZIŊ, mainly between R. Kasaï and R. Kwilu, north of Idiofa;
  MBUUN, east of R. Kwilu in the region of Kikwit, and as far east as R. Longe;
  YEEI;
  and many others.

†DJI̧A and SAKATA, originally placed in this Group (MG2), belong to the MONGO-NKUNDO Group, but have the phonology of TEKE. See p. 48.

NGUL SINGLE UNIT?

MG, 1957

NGUL (j-)   (B.66)

Where spoken: C.B., south of R. Kasaï near its confluence with R. Kamtsha.

Information on this language is still very slight, but it certainly does not belong to the TEKE-YANS Group. It is therefore tentatively classed as a Single Unit.[1]

---

[1] MG, personal communication, 1957.

(33)

NGANDO GROUP

Where spoken: O.-C.

NBi		MG3	Other names
ƊGANDƟ (ɗi-)	50a		Bodzanga, Bangandou, Bagandou[1]
KƟTA (ɗi-)	50b		Bakota
†MBATƗ	51	(MBATI C.13/o) (Sub-Bantu)	Isongo, Lissongo

ƊGANDƟ (ɗi-)

Where spoken: Rég. Lobaye, D. Mbaïki, on the right bank of R. Lobaye, 17° 40'–18° E.
Number: See under KƟTA.

KƟTA (ɗi-)

Where spoken: Rég. Lobaye, D. Mbaïki, on the right bank of R. Lobaye, 17° 30'–17° 40' E.
Number: ƊGANDƟ and KƟTA 2,873 (*Rapport politique*, Lobaye, 1949).
These two dialects are almost identical. The name BODZANGA is also applied to both.

†MBATƗ

Where spoken: Rég. Lobaye, D. Mbaïki and D. Boda, on the left bank of R. Lobaye, 17° 25'–18° 10' E., extending north at one point as far as 4° 10' N.
Number: Mbaïki 15,208, Boda 241 (*Rapport politique*).
Classed in MG2, on the evidence of Ouzilleau's material,[2] in the 'NGUNDI' Group (see PANDE, p. 34). According to NB II ƊGANDƟ shows considerable affinities with MBATƗ, and the BAKƟTA claim to understand MBATƗ, which gives 'the general impression ... that it was produced by the impact of a non-Bantu people from the north-east on a pure Bantu language of the ƊGANDƟ type'.
The MBATƗ claim to have come from C.B. less than a century ago, and that there exists across the Oubangui a language which they understand. MBATƗ appears to be an ancestral name (NBi).[3]

[1] ƊGANDƟ must be distinguished from ƊGANDO of C.B. (see MONGO-NKUNDU Group, p. 48), and from 'N. BANGANTU' (BAAGƏTO) (see MAKAA Group, p. 19) and 'S. BANGANTU' (non-Bantu); KƟTA must be distinguished from KOTA of M.-C. and G. (see KOTA Group, p. 24).
[2] 'Notes sur la langue des Pygmées de la Sanga.'
[3] Note that MBATI or MBAATI appears to be the ancestral name of the people in C.B. who now speak NGBANDI (non-Bantu). See NBii, p. 102.

PANDE GROUP[1]

Where spoken: O.-C. and M.-C. also perhaps C.B.

MG3		NBi		Other names
NGONDI	C.11/*	ƊGONDI	49b	Ngundi
⎧PANDE	C.12/0	PANDE (i-ʃande)	49	Ndjeli, Linyeli, Linzeli
⎩BOGƆNGƆ	C.12/*	BOGƆƊGƆ	49c	Bukongo, Bongili, Bongiri
†MBATI	C.13/0			
But see NGANDO Group, p. 33.				
MBOMOTABA	C.14/*			Bamitaba
BONGILI	C.15/*			Bongiri, Bungiri
				Also perhaps (NBii):
				NDAANDA (Kpala)
				LOBALA
				BOMBOLI (Bombongo)

Of this Group, NBi states: 'It was found impossible to obtain conclusive evidence regarding the languages of this group, owing to (i) the very nature of this sparsely populated, inaccessible, and largely unknown forest region, (ii) the confusion of names of speeches and localities which exists, not only amongst Europeans but also in the minds of neighbouring Africans.'

The name PANDE seems to be used as a general term, synonymous with NDJƐLI and including 'all those languages which are felt to be "similar", i.e. ƊGONDI, "PANDE proper", BOGƆƊGƆ, and perhaps others which have up to now been miscalled PANDE, &c.' (NBi).

The name MBUNDJO has been applied to some Bantu languages of southern M.-C., and also to the non-Bantu language spoken along the right bank of the Oubangui immediately to the south of the MONDJOMBO, whose speech it closely resembles (NB II).

ƊGONDI

Where spoken: O.-C., in fishing villages along R. Sangha between Nola and Bayanga.

MG's material was recorded at Nola, and shows this language to be Sub-Bantu, and closely related to 'PANDE'. It appears, however, that there may be two different languages, both known as NGONDI, of which the second (IƊGONDI), spoken at Ngoundi and Ndélé on R. Lobaye is that recorded by NBi, and appears to consist of a mixture of PANDE and non-Bantu GBAYA, GBOFI, ALI, and NGBAKA MABO, with a preponderance of non-Bantu vocabulary. This would explain why 'the wildest statements were made concerning interintelligibility' (NBi).

PANDE (i-)

Where spoken: O.-C., Rég. Haute-Sangha, D. Berbérati at Bania on R. Mambéré, also round Nola; Rég. Lobaye, D. Boda, round Bambio and Boungué on R. Mbaéré,

[1] The name PANDE is here used as the Group name, instead of MG3's NGUNDI.

PANDE GROUP

and at Ndio on R. Bodengué; M.-C., D. Dongou at Ancien Béra Njoko on R. Ibengué (by the KODGWALA) and at Makaou on R. Motaba (by people known as IKƐDGA) (NBi).

Number: D. Boda 1,000 (*Rapport politique*).

BǪGƆNGƆ

Where spoken: O.-C., Rég. Haute-Sangha, D. Berbérati, in several villages on the Bania–Nola road.

This is the BONGIRI referred to by Bruel.[1]

MBǪMǪTABA

Where spoken: M.-C., in isolated groups in the swampy forest between R. Sangha and R. Oubangui, north-east of Ikélemba.

MG[2] describes MBǪMǪTABA as a collection of dialects, probably of common origin, which are not interintelligible, though their speakers all claim the name MBǪMǪTABA.

BǪNGĮLĮ

Where spoken: M.-C., west of R. Sangha downstream from Ouesso and Ikélemba.

The following speeches in C.B., Terr. Bomboma, are tentatively placed in this Group on geographical grounds. They are said to be perhaps related to 'the languages of the right bank of the Ubangi' (NBii).

NDAANDA (the speakers are called KPALA by the Bomboli).

LOBALA, spoken in an area adjacent to the MONJOMBO.

BOMBOLI, a dialect of LOBALA (but see also under NGIRI in NGALA Group, p. 37).

---

[1] *L'Afrique Équatoriale Française* (1918).   [2] Personal communication.

MBOSHI GROUP

Where spoken: M.-C.

MG3		Other names
MBOKO	C.21/o	
AKWA	C.22/*	
NGARE	C.23/o	
KOYO	C.24/*	
MBƆSI	C.25/*	Mboshi
KWALA (lj-)	C.26/*	Likwala, Likouala
KUBA (lj-)	C.27/*	

'Apart from the nucleus of items common to most Bantu languages, the vocabularies of this group appear to contain many peculiar items ... this group is very much one on its own' (MG2).

MBOKO
Where spoken: In the region of Odzala.

AKWA
Where spoken: In the region of Makoua.

NGARE
Where spoken: West of Makoua.

KOYO
Where spoken: In the region of Fort Rousset.

MBƆSI
Where spoken: On both banks of R. Alima south of Fort Rousset.

KWALA (lj-)
Where spoken: Mainly to the west of the lower reaches of R. Likouala.

KUBA (lj-)
Where spoken: On both sides of the lower reaches of R. Alima.

(37)

NGALA GROUP

Where spoken: C.B.

MG3		NBii		Other names
		MABAALE W.A. I: 1		Mabale
		MABAALE(lo-)	a	
		BEMBE	b	BƐMBƐ (H50)
		LIPANJA		
		BANZA	c	
		MBINGA	d	
		LOBO	e	BALƆBƆ (H50)—see under NGIRI below.
		BAALI (di-)	2	
		But see NGOMBE Group, p. 43.		
		BOKO	3	
(BOLOKI— see below)	C.36e	BOLOKI	4	Bologi, Buluki
		NDOOBO	5	Ndobo
		? LIKILA	6	Bangele, Balobo
NGIRI	C.31b/o	NGIRI W.A. II:		NGIRI (H50):
		LIBINZA	1	LIBINJA
		But see NGOMBE Group.		
LƆI	C.31a/*	LOI	2	BALOI, Rebu
NUNU	C.31c/o			MAMPOKO
				JAMBA-MAKUTU
				MANGANJI
				BOMBOLI
				See also PANDE Group, p. 34.
				BALƆBƆ—see above;
				NDOLO—see under 'Saw' below;
				and many others.
BOBANGI	C.32/*			Bobangi, Bangi, Rebu
		'Saw' W.A. III:		
		BOLONDO	1	
		NDOOLO	2	—see under NGIRI above.
SƐNGƐLƐ (kɛ-)	C.33/*			
†BOLIA	C.34/o			

See also MONGO-NKUNDO Group, p. 48.

NGALA GROUP

MG3		NBii		Other names
†NTǪMBA (lǫ-) C.35/*				Lontomba
See also MONGO-NKUNDO Group p. 48.				
LǪSƐNGƆ C.36:				LƆSƐDGƆ (H50), Lusengo
⎧ PƆTƆ (li̧-) C.36a/*	UPOTO	W.C. II. 6		PƆTƆ (H50)
⎪	⎧ POTO (li-)	a		
⎪	⎪ KELE	b		
⎪	⎪ POTO 'BUMWANGI	c		
⎨ MPƐSA (li̧-) C.36b/*	⎨ POTO EMPESA	d		
⎪	⎪ NGUNDJI (i-)	e		
⎪	⎪ Kunda and Kumba	f		
⎪	⎪ Mongo	g		
⎪	⎪ Terr. Busu Djanga	h		
⎪	⎪ Esumba	i		
⎪	⎪ POTO (Mongala)	j		
⎪	⎩ POTO (Lusengo)	k		
⎪ MBŲDZA C.36c/* (li̧-)				
⎪ MANGALA C.36d/* (LINGALA)				NGALA: ⎧ LINGALA ⎨ BANGALA ⎩ MANGALA
⎪ BǪLǪKI̧ C.36e/*—see above.				
⎪ KANGANA C.36f/o				
⎩ LƐKǪ (ę-) C.36g/o				Eleko, Lεku (lo-)
and probably many others.[1]				
BŲJA (i-) C.37/*				
But see NGOMBE Group, p. 43.				
	BASOA- BASOKO	W.C. II. 1		BASƆKƆ (H50)
	But see SƆ in KELE Group (p. 46).			
	See also MONGO-NKUNDO Group, p. 48.			
	BAONGA	2		
	YAMONGERI	3		
	R. Congo villages	4		
(MBƐSA C.51/o)	MBESA (u-)			Mombesa
See KELE Group, p. 46.				
				ŊGƐLƐ of Irebu (H50)

Note: There is considerable overlapping of names between this and other neighbouring Groups, e.g.:
di-BAALI, cp. WIINZA-DIBALI in NGOMBE Group.
LIBINZA, also in NGOMBE Group.

[1] MG, personal communication.

NGALA GROUP

MG3 groups BỤJA in this Group, NBii has a sub-group BUDJA in the 'NGOMBE bloc'.

BOLIA and NTỌMBA are described by Hulstaert as MONGO influenced by Congo riverine languages.

MABAALE (lo-)

Where spoken: On R. Congo in the Nouvelle Anvers area:

(a) lo-MABAALE, at Nouvelle Anvers;
(b) BEMBE and LIPANJA, east and west of Nouvelle Anvers respectively;
(c) BANZA, opposite Nouvelle Anvers;
(d) MBINGA, in four villages on the right bank of R. Congo;
(e) LOBO, spoken by the BALOBO, comprising the BODJINGA in the north, BOKULA in the centre, and BONKEMBE in the south.

BAALI (di-)

Where spoken: On R. Dua in Terr. Busu Mandji.

BOKO

Where spoken: Nouvelle Anvers, and Dundu on the right bank.

BỌLỌKỊ

Where spoken: In riverside villages downstream from the MABAALE area; also farther upstream.

Hulstaert points out that this language (believed, however, by MG to be extinct) must be distinguished from the language of the BOLOKI of R. Ruki (for which, see MONGO-NKUNDO Group, p. 48).

NDOOBO

Where spoken: Along Ndobo stream and on R. Congo north of the BOLOKI area.

LIKILA

Where spoken: In four villages between R. Ubangi and R. Congo.

This language, known to neighbouring peoples as BANGELE or BALOBO, is perhaps related to the above.

All the above languages and/or dialects constitute the 'Congo River sub-group' of the Western Sector of the Western Group of NBii.

NGỊRỊ

Where spoken: In the R. Ngiri area. The name is used in NBii to cover LIBINZA and LƆỊ (see below).

LIBINZA

Where spoken: On R. Ngiri and in two villages on R. Congo.

LƆỊ

Where spoken: M.-C. and C.B. on both sides of R. Ubangi, from R. Sangha in the west to R. Congo in the east, and northwards almost from the Ubangi mouth to 0° 30′ N.; also along the middle Ngiri.

NGALA GROUP

The speakers are called BA-LOI or 'BAATO 'BA LOI (i.e. people of the Ngiri) (NBii).

H51 describes LOI as intermediate between BANGI (see below) and the speech of R. Ngiri.

NUNU is listed in MG3 in the same Dialect Cluster.

For other names given by H50 under NGIRI see list above. He describes the NGIRI 'group' as a 'Substrat Mɔngɔ' with NGOMBE influence.

BOBANGI

Where spoken: In the Bolobo–Irebu–Stanley Pool area, and on some islands in the river; also spoken by riverine peoples between Irebu and the Kasaï confluence, and on the lower Ubangi near the Ngiri confluence (H51).

Used as a medium of communication as far east as L. Léopold II, and in substandard education in mission schools.

The 'Saw' group on R. Saw (NBii) consists of two units:

BOLONDO

Where spoken: On R. Saw south of Budjala.
Number: c. 1,000.

NDOOLO

Where spoken: In the Ndoolo marshes between Bokola and Tanda.
Number: c. 5,000.

Spoken by people of various origins who are collectively known as 'BONDOKOYI (NBii).

The speech of Likula on R. Mongala is perhaps also related.

SƐNGƐLƐ (ke-)

Where spoken: From the western shore of L. Léopold II north-westwards to within about 20 miles of R. Congo.

Used in mission work.

†BOLIA

Where spoken: Between L. Léopold II and L. Tumba, extending a little way both east and west.

According to H51 closely related to NTOMBA (see below).

†NTOMBA (lo-)

Where spoken: North-east of L. Tumba.
Number: 40,000–50,000 (H. D. Brown).[1]

According to H51 belongs to the MONGO-NKUNDO Group, but has been influenced by Congo riverine languages.

LOSƐNGƆ. This name, which is geographical only, and not a tribal or linguistic name, has been chosen by MG to cover a number of dialects.

---

[1] 'The Nkumu of the Tumba...' (*Africa*, 1944).

PƆTƆ (li-) (MG3) is roughly identical with the 'various dialects included under the common name of Upoto' in NBii (in the Eastern Sector of the Western Group):
POTO (li-) of Bumba;
KELE of Umangi;
POTO 'BUMWANGI of Umangi;
POTO EMPESA (the MPƐSA of MG3);
NGUNDJI (i-), opposite Umangi;
the speech of Kunda and Kumba near Boyange;
the speech of Mongo below Lisala;
the speech of Yakata, Yamongeri, Liombe, and Yambuya in Terr. Busu Mandji;
the speech of Esumba Island opposite Umangi;
POTO, above the mouth of R. Mongala;
POTO of Lusengo below the mouth of R. Mongala.

MBŲDZA (li-)
Where spoken: In fishing villages on both banks of R. Congo west of Lisala.

NGALA

This name is used in so many different senses (with various prefixes) that it appears to have no precise significance. The following may be distinguished:

LINGALA. Used as a lingua franca on both sides of R. Congo from Léopoldville to Basoko; it is the medium of primary education in many centres in the area, and is the official language of the 'Force Publique', &c.

H50 distinguishes between:
'LINGALA scolaire', as used in education, and
'LINGALA populaire', used by officials.

The speech of the Lisala area is regarded by both missionaries and officials as being the 'best' form (Tucker).[1]

BANGALA, an attenuated form of LINGALA, is widely used as a trade language among Bantu and non-Bantu speakers of the northern part of C.B.

MANGALA is in common use in C.B. and in parts of M.-C., among speakers of various small languages and dialects (e.g. the MBǪMǪTABA, who 'are forced by the extreme localization of their dialects to speak together in MANGALA' (MG, quoted in NBi). MANGALA has developed by attrition, and later by accretion, from BOLOKI.[2]

In DB it is stated that 'Ngala as a pure Bantu tongue is spoken on the north and south banks of the Congo River between 18° 30' and 21° East longitude. This language is today called "Lingala", though it is based on the speech of the Mangala people'. In NBii, however, it is stated that 'despite all our researches in this region, we were unable to find a tribe bearing the ethnic name of Bangala or Bamangala; nor did we find a village-language called Lingala'.

[1] Personal communication.
[2] See Guthrie, 'The Lingua Franca of the Middle Congo' (*Africa*, 1943).

NGALA GROUP

MG3 further includes in his LƆSƐNGƆ Cluster:
BOLOKỊ (see above);
KANGANA (locality unknown; noted by Johnston);
LẸKƆ (ẹ-), almost extinct, spoken on R. Tshuapa and around Lolanga.

BỤJA (ẹ-)

Where spoken: In a belt about 50 miles wide just north of R. Congo between the Itimbiri confluence and Lisala.

Number: *c.* 100,000 (VBRL, quoting van Houteghen).

Classed in the NGOMBE Group in NBii (see p. 43).

The following are placed in the Western Group (Southern Sector) of NBii.

The speech of the BASOA-BASOKO.

Where spoken: On the right bank of R. Congo, at Yambese and Basoa; Yoafo and Basoko at the mouth of R. Aruwimi; Bomenge and villages of the lower R. Lulu; one village on the left bank in Terr. Isangi.

(But see SƆ in KELE Group, p. 46, and note on SOKO in the MONGO-NKUNDO Group, p. 48.)

The speech of the BAONGA

Where spoken: In one village on the left bank in Terr. Isangi.

The speech of the YAMONGERI

Where spoken: At Yaolema.

The speech of four villages on R. Congo east of the mouth of R. Itimbiri.

MBESA (u-)

Where spoken: On the left bank of R. Congo, opposite the YAMONGERI.
Classed in the KELE Group (p. 46) by MG3.

H50 also adds:

ŊGƐLƐ of Irebu.

NGOMBE GROUP

Where spoken: C.B.

In NBii an enormous number of dialects is listed under the general heading 'Northern Group'. Only the names given as headings of sub-groups are given here, together with such names as also occur in the writings of other authorities. The 'Western Group Transition Languages' of NBii are added to this Group, following H50. For further details the reader is referred to NBii, pp. 76–81 and 73–74.

NBii		MG3		H50	Other names
KUNDA	Northern A.				
'NGOMBE Bloc'	B.				
⎧NGOMBE	I a–c	NGƆMBƐ (lj-)	C.41/*		
⎪BUDJA	II a–c	(BỤJA (e̩-)	C.37/*)	EMB	
⎪BINZA	III a–g				
⎪ including					
⎨⎧BINZA (li-). But see NGALA Group, p. 37.				BINJA	
⎪⎪BINDJA (li-)					
⎪⎨GENDJA (di-)				GENJA	
⎪⎪GENDZA-BAALI. But see NGALA Group.					
⎩⎩WIINZA-BAALI. But see NGALA Group.					
'DOKO	W. Tr. A. 1–2			DƆKƆ	
TEMBO (li-)	B.				
'DOKO of Ngiri	C. 1–5			DIANGA	
		BWƐLA (lj-)	C.42/o	BUELA	Lingi
'BWA Bloc'	Northern C.				
⎧'APAGIBETI'	I a–f				Gezon
⎪BENGE-BAATI	II a–d				
⎪ ('NAPAGISENE'), including					
⎪ BENGE (li-)					Libenge
⎪ BAATI (li-)		BATỊ (lj-)	C.43/o		lɛ-ɓaatẹ (Tucker)[1]
⎪'NAPAGIBETINI'	III a–f				
⎨YEWU	IV a–c				
⎪ ('NAPAGIBETINI')					
⎪BWA	V a–f	BƠA (lj-)	C.44/o		Bali, Bango
⎪ ('NAPAGITENE')					Libwali
⎪'Pseudo-BANGE-					
⎪ LIMA'	VI a–h, including				
⎪ ⎧BORO (le-)					Buru
⎩ ⎩ANGBA (le-)		AƊBA (li-)	C.45/o		Ngelima, Beo, Tungu
KANGO (li-)	Northern D. I–V				

[1] Personal communication.

NGOMBE GROUP

KUNDA, spoken by 'a group of pseudo-riverines' who call themselves KUNDA.
Where spoken: On R. Saw and R. Ngiri.

The 'NGOMBE Bloc'

NGƆMBƐ (lį-)

Where spoken: Over a wide area: (*a*) (Northern NGOMBE) in an enclave around Bosobolo, and in five small enclaves in Terr. Libenge; (*b*) (R. Congo NGOMBE) on the left bank of R. Congo from 19° 10′ E. to beyond Lisala, on the right bank around Lisala, and farther west; between R. Congo and R. Mongala; between R. Saw and R. Ngiri; north of Bomboma; in Mawuya region of Terr. Libenge (MBATI-NGOMBE); (*c*) Terr. Busu Mandji, Lisala, and Budjala.
Number: *c*. 150,000.
Used in sub-standard education.

BỤJA (e-). See NGALA Group, p. 37.

BINZA (li-)

Where spoken: (*a*) On R. Dua in Yambuku and Busu Mandji areas; (*b*) in Boyange area, Terr. Lisala; (*c*) north of R. Itimbiri in the Aketi area, and south of R. Itimbiri round Ibembo and to the south-east; (*d*) farther south-east, extending to R. Aruwimi.
'This is an immense group, the various dialects of which we found exceedingly difficult to classify' (NBii).
See also NGALA Group, p. 37.

H50 further adds to NGOMBE, the 'Western Transition Languages' of NBii:

'DOKO

Where spoken: In the Lisala–Busu Mandji–R. Mongala area, and in Terr. Budjala.

TEMBO (li-)

Where spoken: Widely scattered on R. Mongala, on islands in R. Congo, and in enclaves to the north.

'DOKO of R. Ngiri.

Where spoken: Terr. Bomboma.

DIANGA (no location given).

BWƐLA

Where spoken: On the right bank of R. Congo and on R. Mongala. According to H51 the BUELA are a subdivision of the DOKO.

The 'BWA Bloc'

The 'investigation of the Bobwa (popularly known as Ababua) was rendered especially difficult by the extreme multiplicity of their languages, which have not only been superimposed but often completely intermingled' (NBii).

NGOMBE GROUP

In the absence of any discoverable group name, these dialects have been grouped together in NBii often under a name which 'refers neither to a language nor to a clan, but is merely a cognomen given to these people who habitually begin a conversation with the formula "He says that ... *apa-gi-beti* ..." ' (NBii).

'APAGIBETI' dialects
Where spoken: In the R. Dua–Abumombazi area; between R. Uele and R. Likati (spoken by, among others, the ba-BOGULU);[1] in the northern part of Terr. Lisala.

BENGE-BAATI ('NAPAGISENE'), including:
BENGE (li-)
Where spoken: North of R. Uele; between R. Uele and R. Likati; in the Aketi–Ibembo area north of R. Itimbiri.

BAATI (li-)
Where spoken: Much scattered, in three areas between R. Likati and R. Itimbiri, and north of R. Rubi.

'NAPAGIBETINI' dialects (a 'transition group')
Where spoken: West of R. Soombo and in the Ngayi and Likati areas; south of R. Bima in the Berisi–Titule area; between R. Rubi and R. Tely and south of the Tely.

YEWU ('NAPAGIBETINI') dialects
Where spoken: between R. Bima and R. Ombo.

BWA ('NAPAGITENE') dialects
Where spoken: Between R. Bima and R. Uele.

Dialects of the 'Pseudo-BANGELIMA', including:
BORO (le-)
ANGBA (le-)
Where spoken: Mainly in Terr. Banalia.

KANGO (li-)
The fisherfolk of the lower Uele, the Api, Bima, and Bomokandi all call themselves ba-KANGO. 'They all claim to speak Likango but the diversity of these languages shows that this name merely designates a medium of intercomprehension obtained by deliberately deforming and degrading their various forms of speech' (i.e. 'APAGIBETI', BENGE-BAATI, YEWU, and BWA) (NBii).

[1] e-gɔtɔ, spoken by the бǫ-gɔtɔ (Tucker, personal communication). To be distinguished from the BOGURU dialects (see p. 86).

KELE GROUP[1]

Where spoken: C.B.

MG3		NBii	Other names
MBƐSA	C.51/o		
But see NGALA Group, p. 37.			
†SƆ (hẹ-)	C.52/*		Soko, Eso, Heso, Sɔkɔ
See also BASOA-BASOKO in NGALA Group and SOKO in MONGO-NKUNDO Group, pp. 37, 48.			
PỌKẸ (tọ-)	C.53/*	TOPOKE N. Trans., B. I	Tofoke
		LIUTWA IIa	
		BALUOMBILA IIb	
		(A)LOMBOOKI III	
		LIKOLO IV	
LỌMBỌ (ọ-)	C.54/*	OLOMBO N. Trans. A. I–III	ỌLỌMBỌ (Tucker),[2] Turumbu
KẸLẸ (ẹ-)	C.55/*	KELE W. B. 1–3	Lokele
		⎧YAWEMBE 1a	
		⎪YAOKANDJA 1b	
		⎨MBOOSO 2	
		⎪YALIKOKA	
†FƆMA (lị-)	C.56/o	⎩FUMA 3	pseudo-Bambole
See also MONGO-NKUNDO Group.			

SƆ (hẹ-)

Where spoken: On both banks of the lower Aruwimi.

Note: According to H50 the area occupied by the SƆ is smaller than that shown on the map in MG1.

Number: c. 6,000.

In NBii the speech of the BASOA-BASOKO is classed with other dialects in the NGALA Group. According to H51 SƆKƆ is 'close to KELE and to several MƆNGƆ dialects'.

PỌKẸ (TOPOKE)

Where spoken: In a belt about 60 miles wide, slightly inland from the left bank of R. Lomami from the equator to the Congo confluence, and westwards along the left bank of the Congo to 23° 20′ E.

According to H51 the TOPOKE occupy the area shown as NGANDU on the map in MG1.

Number: 45,958 (NBii).

---

[1] Called SOKO-KELE Group in MG3. The name used here is that of the best-known unit in the Group.
[2] Personal communication.

KELE GROUP

According to NBii TOPOKE is spoken by:
'TOPOKE proper', in Terr. Isangi.
LIUTWA and BALUOMBILA (probably of non-TOPOKE origin.
(A)LOMBOOKI ('pseudo-LOKELE') of R. Lomami. They do not accept the name LOKELE or TOPOKE. Their speech shows (*a*) a vocabulary which is basically TOPOKE, with loan-words from the MONGO area; (*b*) LOKELE influence in the verbal system.
LIKOLO, in Yangongo area.

OLOMBO (TURUMBU)

Where spoken: Terr. Isangi, mainly on the right bank of R. Congo near the riverine KELE; also in a few villages on the left bank, among the KELE.
Number: 10,395 (NBii).
The 'TURUMBU de l'eau' or YANONGO of Elisabetha perhaps no longer speak TURUMBU (NBii).

KELE (e-) (LOKELE)

Where spoken: On both banks of R. Congo and R. Lomami from their confluence (*a*) to within 10 miles of Stanleyville; (*b*) almost to the equator.
Number: c. 14,000 (NBii); 26,000 (Carrington).[1]
Two dialects are distinguished in NBii:
Western, spoken by the YAWEMBE, mainly in the neighbourhood of Yangambi and Isangi;
Eastern, spoken by the YAOKANDJA in the neighbourhood of Yakusu and Yanonge.
The LILEKO on the left bank of R. Congo speak LOKELE and there are several other settlements further downstream, e.g. in Terr. Bumba and Lisala.
LOKELE is also spoken by:
MBOOSO, on the right bank of R. Lomami opposite Isangi;
YALIKOKA, south of the above. Of TOPOKE origin.
Number: 6,902 together.
†FUMA (FƆMA), also known as 'pseudo-BAMBOLE' (see MBOLE in MONGO-NKUNDO Group, p. 48).
KELE is used in sub-standard and religious education over a wide area, among tribes who speak related languages.

[1] 'The Tonal Structure of Kele (Lokele)' (*Afr. Stud.*, 1944).

(48)

MONGO-NKUNDO GROUP

Where spoken: C.B.

	MG3		H50, 51	NBii	Other names
MƆNGƆ-NKỤNDỌ	C.61:				
⎧ MƆNGƆ (lọ-)	C.61a/*	MƆNGƆ			Lomongo
⎪ NKỤNDỌ (lọ-)	C.61b/*	ŊKUNDO			Lonkundu, Lolo
⎪ WANGATA	C.61c/o				
⎨ MPAMA	C.61d/o	MPAMA			
⎪ 'S. NKỤNDỌ'	C.61e/o:¹				
⎪ ⎧ PANGA (i-)					
⎪ ⎪ TỊTỤ		TITU			
⎪ ⎨ BUULỊ		ƆLI			
⎪ ⎪ BUKALA		KALA			
⎩ ⎩ YAILIMA		YAJIMA			
and others					
		EKONDA			
		BAKUTU			
		BO-LƆŊGƆ			
NGANDỌ	C.63/*	ŊGANDO			
LALỊA	C.62/o	LALIA			
†(MBƆLƐ	D.11/o)	MBƆLƐ	MBOLE (lo-)	N. Trans. C.	
See MBOLE-ENA Group?, p. 103.					
			⎧ KEEMBO	I	
			⎪ YAAMBA	II	
			⎨ YAISU, &c.	III	
†(FƆMA (lị-)	C.56/o)		⎩ FUMA	IV	
See also KELE Group, p. 46.					
		INJA			
		ŊKEMBE(lo-)			
†(NTỌMBA	C.35/*)	NTOMBA(lo-)			Lontomba
See NGALA Group, p. 37.					
		⎧ ŊKƆLƐ			
		⎪ IMOMA			
		⎨ MPOŊGO			
		⎩ ŊKƆLƐ of			
		R. Ruki			
†(BỌLỊA	C.34/o)	BOLIA			
See NGALA Group.					
		BOLOKI of			
		R. Ruki			
		SAKAN(Y)I			
		SOKO			

See also SƆ in KELE Group, &c.

¹ List of dialects from MG1.

MONGO-NKUNDO GROUP

	MG3		Other names
†(ɔMBɔ		C.76/o)	OMBO, lɔ-ɔmbɔ,[1] Hombo, Songola

See also TETELA Group.

† { DJĮA (ki-)   (B.84/*)
    SAKATA (ki-)

See also TEKE-YANS Group, p. 29.

VBRL and H51 also include the TETELA (C.70) and KUBA (C.80) Groups of MG, and VBRL adds SƐNGƐLƐ, for which see NGALA Group, p. 37.

H50 further draws attention to the close affinity of KELE and MONGO, 'de sorte que, à notre avis, il pourrait être uni à celui-ci'—but he also refers to 'divergences notables'.

MONGO-NKUNDO dialects

Where spoken: Over a vast area bounded in the north and west by riverine and lacustrine settlements of R. Congo and L. Tumba and L. Léopold II, in the southwest by R. Lukenie, and extending as far as 23° E.

MƆNGƆ (lo̧-)

Where spoken: In the north-eastern part of the total area.
Number: 80,000 (van der Kerken).
Used in sub-standard education and religious instruction.

NKU̧NDO̧ (lo̧-)

Where spoken: In the southern part of the total area.
Number: 130,619 (1937 Census, quoted VBRL).
Used in sub-standard education and religious instruction.

WANGATA

Where spoken: West of L. Tumba.

MPAMA

Where spoken: North-west of L. Tumba.
Number: 6,000 (VBRL).

These two dialects were classed in Group C.20 (NGALA) in MG1, but are now placed in this Group (MG3).

'S. NKU̧NDO̧', a name used in MG3 to cover various little-known dialects, including:
PANGA (i-), *c.* 19° 30′ E.;
TJTU̧, *c.* 20° E.;
BUULJ, 19° 30′–20° 30′ E., in a belt about 50 miles wide on the north bank of R. Kasaï;
BUKALA, *c.* 20° 20′ E.;
YAILIMA, *c.* 20° 40′ E.

---

[1] Meeussen, *Esquisse de la langue Ombo* (1952), and personal communication.

H50 further adds:
EKONDA;
the speech of the BAKUTU of Boende;
LƆŊGƆ.

NGANDO

Where spoken: Around the headwaters of R. Lopori and R. Maringa, 1° N.–1° S., 23°–24° E.
Number: 120,590 (Hulstaert).[1]
According to H51 this is a divergent MƆŊGƆ dialect, perhaps including:
LALIA
Where spoken: Between R. Maringa and R. Tshuapa.
Number: 30,000 (VBRL).

†MBƆLƐ

Where spoken: On both banks of R. Lomami from 1° 30′ S. to the equator; to the north-east a belt about 40 miles wide extends to Stanleyville.
Number: 90,000–100,000 (van der Kerken).
MG1, whose authorities are Johnston and Carrington, classes this language in a different Zone, together with other dialects (for which, however, see LEGA Group, p. 92). H51 classes it in the MONGO-NKUNDO Group and in NBii it constitutes part of the 'Northern Group Transition Languages', in which there is much KELE influence.
The MBƆLƐ dialects noted in NBii (south to north) are:
KEEMBO of Opale;
  the speech of the YAAMBA;
  the speech of the YAISU and YAIKOLE, YANGONDA and BOTUNGA, and several 'clans';
  †FUMA, spoken by the YALIHILA and YALIKANDJA—so strongly influenced by KELE that 'the MBOLE substratum has almost disappeared' (see KELE Group, p. 46).
H51 also includes under MBOLE:
INJA;
ŊKEMBE.

†NTOMBA—see NGALA Group, p. 37. Considered by Hulstaert as belonging to the MONGO-NKUNDO Group and including:
ŊKƆLƐ;
IMOMA;
MPOŊGO of R. Luilaka;
ŊKƆLƐ of R. Momboyo-Ruki.

†BOLIA—see NGALA Group.
H51 adds to this Group:
BOLOKI of R. Ruki;
SAKAN(Y)I.
He describes SOKO (see SƆ in KELE Group) as resembling several MONGO dialects.

[1] 'Les tons en Lonkundu' (*Anthropos*, 1934).

†ɔMBɔ

Where spoken: On R. Lualaba opposite Wayika.

Described by Meeussen[1] as a form of MONGO with TETELA vocabulary affinities, spoken by one part of the people known as SONGOLA (the other part speak BINJA; see LEGA Group, p. 92).

MG3 classes ǪMBǪ in the TETELA Group (see p. 52).

†DJIA (ki-)

Where spoken: North of R. Fimi, west of L. Léopold II.

†SAKATA (ki-)

Where spoken: Between R. Lukenie and R. Kasaï, west of 19° E.

These two dialects, classed in the DZING Group in MG3 (see TEKE-YANS Group, p. 29), belong to the MONGO-NKUNDO Group, though their phonology is TEKE.[2]

[1] Op. cit.   [2] MG, personal communication, 1957.

TETELA GROUP

Where spoken: C.B.

MG3		H50, 51	VBRL	Other names
TƐTƐLA (o-)	C.71/*	TƐTƐLA		Sungu
KỤSỤ	C.72/o	KUSU	KUTSU (lo-)	Kongola, Fuluka
NKỤTỤ	C.73/*	NKUTSHU		Nkucu, Nkutu, Bankutu

See also KUBA Group, p. 54.

{ HAMBA
{ NGONGO
{ KONGOLA-MENO
   and others

{ KALO (lo)
{ ƐLƐMBƐ

SAKA (lo-)

YƐLA (bo-)	C.74/o	YƐLA	YƐLA	Kutu, Boyela
KƐLA (o-)	C.75/*			Kela, Lemba
†ƆMBƆ	C.76/o			

See also MONGO-NKUNDO Group, p. 48.

? LANGA
MBULI
? JƆNGA

TƐTƐLA (o-)

Where spoken: In a belt just north of 5° S. from west of R. Sankuru eastwards across R. Lomami and northwards along the Lomami almost to R. Lualaba.

Number: c. 30,000 (British and Foreign Bible Soc. *Report*, 1956).

Used in sub-standard education and religious instruction.

According to H50 'Les Batɛtɛla sont très apparentés aux Mɔŋgɔ et leur langue appartient au groupe Mɔŋgɔ, dont elle constitue cependant une branche nettement différenciée.'

KỤSỤ

Where spoken: Between the mid-Lomami and Lualaba, 2°–4° 30′ S.

Number: 25,828 (VBRL).

Described by H50 as a dialect of TƐTƐLA.

NKỤTỤ

Where spoken: Around the headwaters of R. Tshuapa and R. Lukenie from 22° 30′ E. in the south-west to R. Lomami in the east, and between 4° and 2° S.

Several dialects are noted in VBRL and H51 (see list above).

YƐLA (bo-)

Where spoken: From the mid-Lomela around Botende eastwards to R. Tshuapa, 1°–2° 20′ S.

Number: 33,000 (Molin).[1]

According to VBRL the speakers call themselves ba-KUTU; their speech differs little from MONGO-NKUNDO.

KƐLA (o-)

Where spoken: On R. Lomela around Lomela and for about 100 miles to the south-west of the river.

Number: 48,439 (Hulstaert); 80,000–100,000 (van der Kerken); 4,339 'KELA proper' (VBRL, from Hemelryck, 1927).

†ƆMBƆ—see also MONGO-NKUNDO Group, p. 48.

To this Group, H50 adds:
? LANGA, spoken between R. Tshuapa and R. Lualaba;
MBULI, spoken in Haute-Tshuapa;
? JƆNGA, spoken in Haute-Tshuapa.

[1] 'Notes sur les Boyela.' (*Congo*, 1933).

KUBA GROUP

Where spoken: C.B.

MG3		Vansina[1] (Tribes)	Other names
		KUBA:	
BỤSHƆƆŊ	C.83/*	⎧MBALA	Mbale, Bushong(o), Mongo, Ganga, Shongo
(NKỤTỤ) See TETELA Group, p. 52.	C.73/*	⎨NKUTSHU:	
		⎰LUKU	
		⎱MBENGI	
DƐNGƐSƐ	C.81/0	NDENGESE and others.	Ndɛngɛse, Ileo
LƐLƐ (usi-)	C.84/0	LELE	
WƆNGƆ	C.85/0	WONGO	Gongo, Tukkongo, Tukongo, Tukungo, Ndjembe
SƆNGƆMENƆ	C.82/0		

Note: VBRL gives a list of names under LUBA (see p. 72); according to Vansina, they are the names of KUBA tribes. They include MBALA, WONGO, and LELE (see above), also:
PIANGA (PANGA), NGENDE, NGOMBE (NGOMBIA), NGONGO, TSHOBWA (SHOBA, SHOBWA), DJEMBE (but see NDJEMBE as a name for WONGO above).

KUBA
Where spoken: Between R. Kasaï and R. Sankuru in the north, Lukebu, Dibese forest, and R. Lombele in the east, R. Lulua and R. Kasaï and 6° in the south, R. Lubue in the west (Vansina).

BỤSHƆƆŊ
Where spoken: In the central plain between R. Sankuru, R. Kasaï, R. Lulua, and R. Lubudi (Vansina).
Number: 28,855 (1937 Census).
According to VBRL the speakers call themselves ba-MONGO, and are nicknamed GANGA ('savages').

NKUTSHU, consisting of:
LUKU and MBENGI, between R. Lubudi and R. Lukiku (Vansina).
But see TETELA Group, p. 52.

DƐNGƐSƐ
Where spoken: On R. Lukenie, 21°–22° 30′ E., northwards to the upper Luilaka, southwards to 3° 40′ S.; according to Vansina along the south bank of R. Sankuru.
Number: 3,793 (1937 Census).

[1] *Les Tribus Ba-Kuba et les peuplades apparentées* (Eth. Survey, 1954).

KUBA GROUP

LƐLƐ (usi-)

Where spoken: Between R. Loange in the west, R. Kasaï in the north and east, and 5° 30' S. in the south (Vansina).
Number: 25,978 (1948 Census).
According to H50, 51, the language is perhaps a variant of KUBA.

WƆNGƆ

Where spoken: On the left bank of R. Loange from 4° 30' S. to the border of Kilembe secteur; also in the southern part of Terr. Basongo and the north-western part of Terr. Tshikapa (Vansina).
Number: Estimated at 1,780 (Vansina); 8,000 (VBRL).
According to H50, 51 the language is perhaps a variant of KUBA.
The people are called ba-KONGO by the Pende, NDJEMBE by the Lele (Vansina).

SƆNGƆMENƆ

Where spoken: Between, but not touching, R. Sankuru and R. Lukenie, 20° 30'–23° E.
Number: 30,000–40,000 (VBRL).

KONGO GROUP OR SINGLE UNIT

Where spoken: M.-C., C.B., A.

Innumerable names have been given by various writers as those of KONGO dialects, or of languages more or less closely related to KONGO; the following is a list rather than a classification, and is based mainly on VBRL (the fullest list), but also on MG3,[1] Hulstaert, Doke, and others, and on personal communication from G. Atkins (here cited as GA).[2]

VBRL		MG3		Other sources, and alternative names
Central				
K. of Mpalabala	1			
K. of Mazinga	2	KONGO (ki-)	H.16g*	C. Congo (Laman)
K. of Mukimvika	3			
MBOMA (ki-)	4			
'KONGO simplifié' (ki-NGOY)	5			
SUUNDI (ki-)	6			Sondi, Nsuundi
NDIBU (ki-)	7			
SOLONGO (ki-)	8			Musserongo; SW. KONGO dialect (GA)
E. Central				
MPAANGU (ki-)	9			
NTAANDU (ki-)	10			
MBAAMBA (ki-)	11			Phaku, Mpako
MPESE (ki-)	12			
LUULA	13			
Southern				
KOONGO (kishi-)	14	KONGO (kiʃi-)	H.16h/*	S. Kongo, Xikongo; SW. KONGO (GA)
{ MBATA (ki-)	15			
{ NZAMBA (ki-)				Nzaamba
ZOOMBO (ki-)	16	ZOMBO (ki-)	H.16k/*	Nzombo
South-Eastern				
KOONGO (ki-)	17			SE. Kongo
SOSO, SOOSO	18			

But see TSOTSO under HUNGU below.

[1] Comprising his Groups H10, H40, and most of H30 and L10.

[2] See also Atkins 'A Demographic Survey of the Kimbundu-Kongo Language Border in Angola' (*Bol. Soc. Geogr. Lisboa*, 1955), and 'An Outline of Hungu Grammar' (in Garcia de Orta, *Revista da Junta das Missões Geográficas e de Investigações do Ultramar*).

KONGO GROUP OR SINGLE UNIT

VBRL		MG3		Other sources, and alternative names
NKANU (ki-)	19			
MBEEKO (ki-)	20			
P(H)ATU (ki-)	21			
Western: Coastal				
VILI (ki-), FIOT	22	VILI (ki-)	H.12/o	
LUANGU (kisi(ma)-)	23			LUANGU (SE. KONGO) (GA)
KOONGO (ka-)	24	W. KONGO (ka-)	H.16a/*	Fiote
Cabinda	25			
Mboka	26	MBOKA	H.15/o	
NDINGI	27	NDINGI	H.14/o	Ndinzi, Ngingi
NGOYO (kisi(ma)-)	28			Woyo
Western: Inland				
YOMBE (ki-)	29	YOMBE (ki-)	H.16b/*	
VUNGUNYA (ki-) ('YOMBE classique')	30			
? MBALA (ki-)	31			Mumbala
North-Western				
KUNYI (ki-)	32	KUNYI	H.13/o	
Northern				
BEEMBE (ki-)	33	BEMBE	H.11/o	
BWEENDE (ki-)	34	BWENDE	H.16c/*	Ngoy, Buende, Fiot
YAKA (ki-) (see also No. 52 below)	35			
GAANGALA (ki-)	36			
DOONDO (ki-)	37			
? KAAMBA (ki-)	38			
North-Eastern				
KOONGO (ki-)	39	NE. KONGO (ki-)	H.16e/*	
LARI (ki-)	40	LAADI	H.16d/o	
MBINSA (ki-)	41			Mbensa
Eastern				
HUNGANA (ki-)	42	HUDANNA (ki-)	H.42/*	Huana, Hungaan
TSAAMBA (ki-)	43			Tsaam
PINDI (ki-)	44			Piindi
PENDE (ki-)	45	PENDE (ki-)	L.11/*	Pɛnde, Pindi, Pinji
KWESE (ki-)	46	KWESE (u-)	L.13/*	Kwɛsɛ, Pindi
†SHINJI (ki-)	47	SHINJI	H.36/o	SHINJI (-)[1] (GA); Xinji, Nungo

See also CHOKWE-LUNDA Group, p. 67.

[1] The symbol (-) denotes zero prefix.

KONGO GROUP OR SINGLE UNIT

VBRL		MG3		Other sources, and alternative names
†NUNGO	48			NUNGO (mi-) (GA); Minungo
See also CHOKWE-LUNDA Group, p. 67.				
†SUKU (ki-)	49	SUKU (ki-)	H.32/o	SUKU (SE. KONGO) (GA)
See also CHOKWE-LUNDA Group.				
MBALA (ki-)	50	MBALA (ki-)	H.41/o	
		E. KONGO (ka-)	H.16f/o	Fiote
NGOONGO	51			
YAKA (ki-)	52[1]	YAKA (ki-)	H.31/*	YAKA (SE. KONGO) (GA)
(see also No. 35 above)				
HOLU (ki-)	54			
But see SAMBA-HOLU Group, p. 65.				
POOMBO (ki-)	55			POMBO (SE. KONGO) (GA) (see under HUNGU below)
SOONDE (ki-)	56			
LUUWA (ki-)	57			
'kiKOONGO simplifié du Kwilu'	58			
		HUNGU	H.33/o	HUNGU (-) (GA); Hungo TSOTSO (-) (GA); Sosso See also VBRL No. 18 above. POMBO (GA) (see VBRL No. 55 above) SE. KONGO (GA): PUNA SW. KONGO (GA): YEMBE BUNDA
		SONGO	H.26/o	SONGU (-) MBANGALA (ci-) See also CHOKWE-LUNDA and KIMBUNDU Groups

[1] No. 53 lacking in VBRL's list on p. 672; YAKA is, however, numbered 53 on p. 373, No. 52 being missing.

KONGO GROUP OR SINGLE UNIT

Other sources, and alternative names
KIMBUNDU of Nambuangongo
See also KI-MBUNDU Group, p. 63.

1[1] KONGO, of Mpalabala.
2 KOONGO, of the Mazinga–Mukimbuku area (Laman's 'Central dialect').
3 The dialect of Mukimvika.
4 MBOMA of Mboma.
5 'KOONGO unifié' or ki-NGOY.
  This is the 'United Kongo' now used for publication of the Scriptures.
6 SUUNDI, in C.B. and M.-C., mainly on the right bank of R. Congo, 13° 40'–14° 20' E.
  VBRL mentions several variants, said to be spoken in M.-C.
7 NDIBU, west of Inkisi at Thysville, Tumba, &c.
8 SOLONGO, along the coast at the estuary of R. Zadi; in Angola, between Ambrizete and Zaïre.
  Number: Angola 1,673 (GA)
9 MPAANGU, at Lemfu mission.
10 NTAANDU, at Kisantu.
11 MBAAMBA, in Angola, around Sanza Pombo.[2]
12 MPESE, at Mpese mission.
13 The speech of the LUULA (*a*) on R. Nzele; (*b*) on R. Lumene. Also spoken by the KUUNDJI and DIKA of R. Kwango and the bu-KANGA of R. Loonso and R. Kondji.
14 KONGO (kishi-), in C.B. and A., on the coast, mainly south of the Congo estuary, but including Boma and Banana in the north; southwards to 7° S., eastwards as far as Bembe.
  GA uses the term 'SW. KONGO' as an alternative to kishi-KONGO to cover a number of dialects roughly west of 15° 20' E.
15 MBATA, on both banks of R. Inkisi south of Bongolo;
  NZAMBA, an 'aberrant dialect', spoken by a few people only (a mixture of MBAATA, MBEEKO, and NKANO) (VBRL).
16 ZOOMBO, in A., north-eastwards from San Salvador into C.B., and southwards almost to Bembe.
  Number: A., *c.* 70,000 (J. Tucker).[3]
  Mainly used by traders along the Tumba–Mani–Léopoldville road (VBRL).
17 KOONGO (SE.), in A.
18 SOSO. This is probably the same as TSOTSO (see below, under HUNGU).
19 NKANU.

[1] The numbers used in VBRL are here repeated in the text to facilitate reference.
[2] Not to be confused with MBAMBA farther south (see KIMBUNDU Group).
[3] *Angola. The Land of the Blacksmith Prince* (1933).

20 The speech of the ba-MBEEKO (a) Southern: between R. Luva and R. Beenge, and south of the LUULA; (b) Northern: in three villages farther north.
21 P(H)ATU, spoken by a small group east of the NKANU.
22 VILI (FIOTE), in M.-C. on the coast between Médingo and Pointe Noire, and inland almost to Makabona and Loudima.
   According to H50 this is not a KONGO dialect.
23 LUANGU, on R. Loango. A small group of LUANGU in Angola, at Pango Aluquêm Post, Concelho dos Dembos, claim to be descendants of the 'FIOTE-speaking LOANGO' of Cabinda. Their speech at the present day, however, resembles HUNGU (see below) (GA).
24 KOONGO (ka-), south of Loango. Closely related to VILI.
25 The dialect of Cabinda.
   Both these dialects are spoken in Angola and C.B., on the coast from 5° 30' to R. Congo, and inland to 13° E. It is possible that they are one and the same, and correspond to MG3's H.16a.
26 MBOKA, in C.B. and Cabinda, between the coast and 13° E., 5°–5° 20' S.
   Used in missions.
27 NDINGI, in C.B. on the coast, in the north-western part of Mayombe on (and across?) the A. border.
28 NGOYO.
29 YOMBE, in C.B. and M.-C., mainly on the right bank of R. Congo and around the estuary (4°–5° 40' S., 13°–13° 40' E.).
30 VUNGUNYA ('ki-YOMBE classique'), originally the speech of the KONGO conquerors, since fostered by missions, and now spoken by about 170,000 people (VBRL). According to H50, however, YƆMBƐ is not a KONGO dialect, but probably a dialect of SUUNDI (but see No. 6 above).
31 ? MBALA. No information is available on this dialect; many of the mi-MBALA now speak 'YOMBE classique'. GA notes the use of the name MUMBALA in A. (Terra Nova chieftainship in Concelho da Dande.) He states that the name does not seem to be used by the natives, and is probably of Portuguese origin.
32 KUNYI, in M.-C. between Makaboma and Loudima. Influenced by TEKE, according to Laman.
33 BEEMBE, in M.-C. around Sibiti. Influenced by TEKE.
34 BWEENDE, in C.B. (and M.-C. ?) between Brazzaville and Luozi, and across 4° N.
   According to VBRL the BWEENDE constitute the northern section of the NGOY (see No. 5 above).
35 YAKA, in M.-C., west and north-west of the above.
36 GAANGALA, in C.B., around Mangeembo.
37 DOONDO, in C.B., around Kengoyi.
38 KAAMBA. No information available.
39 KOONGO (ki-) (NE. KONGO), in C.B., mainly from Léopoldville to Manyanga, almost to the Angola frontier in the south, and eastwards to 16° 20' E.; also spoken west of Brazzaville at Madzia (by immigrants?).
40 LARI, round Brazzaville and Linzolo, westwards to Minduli and north-westwards to Fangala (among the TEKE).
41 MBINSA (a) between Nsanda mission and Kimpansi, R. Ludisi and R. Lukunga

KONGO GROUP OR SINGLE UNIT

(affluents of R. Nsele); (*b*) south of Léopoldville; (*c*) at Brazzaville (where its speakers are known as LADI).

Closely related to LARI, and perhaps only a dialectal variant.

42 HUNGANA, in C.B. on the right bank of R. Kwilu, 4°-5° S., and inland for nearly 50 miles.

43 TSAAMBA, 'dispersed in the region' (VBRL).

44 PINDI.

GA notes: 'The ba-PENDI were dispersed by the COKWE. Formerly on R. Lovua, now on R. Kwilu.'

45 PENDE, in C.B. on both banks of the mid-Kwilu from R. Loange in the east, southwards in a narrow belt along R. Kwenge to 7° S.

Note that MG3 classes both PENDE and KWESE in a different Zone.

46 KWESE, in A. and C.B., on the upper Kwilu (Cuilu).

See note on No. 45 above.

47 †SHINJI, in A., on the east bank of the upper Kwilu, in a belt about 50 miles wide, 8° 30'-10° S.

According to GA this dialect stands between the KONGO and CHOKWE-LUNDA Groups (see also pp. 56, 67).

48 †NUNGO (mi-). According to GA stands between the KONGO and CHOKWE-LUNDA Groups; according to White, however,[1] it should be classed with CHOKWE.

49 †SUKU, in C.B. and A. (*a*) on the east bank of R. Kwango, 7° 30'-8° S.; (*b*) mainly on the west bank of R. Uamba, 5° 30'-7° S.

Number: 74,238 in C.B. (VBRL from 1945 Census).

According to GA it appears to stand between the KONGO and CHOKWE-LUNDA Groups.

50 MBALA, in C.B., in a belt 50-60 miles wide north-west and south-east from R. Kwango at Fombona and Kimbu to R. Kwilu at Banza.

51 NGOONGO.

52 YAKA, in C.B. and A., in the mid-Kwango basin, 4° 30'-7° 20' S., and for about 50 miles on each side of the river.

54 HOLU (see SAMBA-HOLU Group, p. 65).

55 POOMBO, in A., Sanza Pombo. Very closely related to HUNGU (see below).

56 SOONDE.

57 LUUWA.

58 'ki-KOONGO simplifié du Kwilu.'

A mission product, not the lingua franca (VBRL).

To these dialects, GA adds:

HUNGU, in A., in a wedge between the western and eastern sections of the MBUNDU (*a*) in an area bounded in the north by R. Lulova at Ngage, in the south by a line through Bula Atumba–Caculo Cabaça–Samba Caju; (*b*) east of Puri to R. Cuango (Kwango); also in a small enclave near Camabatela.

Number: 61,520 (GA, from Census figures).

[1] Quoted in McCulloch, *The Southern Lunda and Related Peoples* (Eth. Survey, 1951).

These two HUNGU-speaking areas are separated by speakers of dialects which are closely related to HUNGU:

TSOTSO, around Puri.
Number: 6,502 (GA, from Census figures).
POMBO, in Sanza Pombo (see No. 55 above).
The present-day speech of the LUANGU in Pango Aluquêm Post closely resembles HUNGU (the speech of older people was not investigated). See No. 23 above.
Number: 11,425 (GA, from Census figures).
Other KONGO dialects in A. mentioned by GA are:
Under 'SE. KONGO':
PUNA of Uamba.
Under 'SW. KONGO':
YEMBE, between Ambriz and R. Onzo.
Number: 8,734.
BUNDA, farther inland, in Quimbumbe Post.
A dialect resembling the above, locally known by the tribal names SASSU and LUMBO, spoken in Nambuangongo Post.

He also names, as standing between the KONGO and CHOKWE-LUNDA Groups:

†SONGU, at Mussolo, Nova Gaia.

†MBANGALA, near Iongo (it also shows some resemblance to KIMBUNDU).

†KIMBUNDU of Nambuangongo resembles KIMBUNDU in grammatical structure, KONGO in phonology; the vocabulary is mixed (GA). See p. 63.

KONGO, the lingua franca.
Of the lingua franca, KONGO, H50 states that it is known as 'KONGO commercial' or FIOTE, IKELEVE or ki-LETA (i.e. 'langue de l'état'), and is used by Government agents, traders, and settlers in Bas-Kongo and Kwango, also by missions, at least by the Roman Catholic missions in Kwango. It is, however, being supplanted by LINGALA (see p. 41) in some areas. It is described by Swartenbroeckx[1] as being based on ki-SANTU (see NTAANDU, p. 59), with elements of 'FIOTE' (i.e. the debased language of the lower Congo) and of other languages, including European ones.

[1] *Dictionnaire kikongo simplifié–français, français–kikongo simplifié.*

KIMBUNDU SINGLE UNIT[1]

Where spoken: A.

Classification according to G. Atkins.[2]

GA	MG3		Other names
KIMBUNDU:	NDONGO (ki-)	H.21/*	Nbundu, N'Bundo
⎰NGOLA	NGOLA	H.24/o	
⎱NJINGA:			Ginga, Jinga
⎰MBAMBA(ki-)	MBAMBA	H.22/o	Bambeiro
⎱MBAKA			Ambaquista

†KIMBUNDU of Nambuangongo
  See also KONGO Group, p. 56.

†MBANGALA (ci-)
  See also KONGO and CHOKWE-LUNDA Groups, pp. 56, 67.

	SAMA (ki-)	H.23/o	Kissama, Quissama
	BOLO (lu-)	H.25/o	Libolo, Haka
	†SONGO	H.26/o	Nsongo

  See SONGU in KONGO and CHOKWE-LUNDA
  Groups, pp. 58, 67.

? DONGO, NDONGO
  See also SAMBA-HOLU Group, p. 65.
  Other names used by various writers are given below.

Note on the name NDONGO.

This name has been used by DB for the whole KIMBUNDU Cluster. The DONGO or NDONGO were formerly a famous tribe and the name occurs in writings from the seventeenth century onwards. No trace of these people is now to be found except in three villages in Forte República Post (not enumerated in the Census). It is not even known whether they speak KIMBUNDU, or HOLU (as suggested by HOLU informants) (GA).

KIMBUNDU

Where spoken: Northern Angola, south of 8° S. approx.
Used in religious instruction.
There are two main dialects:

NGOLA

Where spoken: In the western part of the area.
Number: 40,965 (GA, from Census figures).

---

[1] The name is here used with prefix (**ki-**) in order to distinguish it from **u**-MBUNDU farther south (see p. 158). The name MBUNDU does not appear to be in use as a tribal designation (Atkins, quoting A. de Assis Junior, *Dicionário Kimbundu–Português*).

[2] 'A demographic survey . . .' and personal communication.

NJINGA
> *Where spoken*: In the eastern part of the area.
> *Number*: 70,601 (GA, from Census figures).
> Under the heading NJINGA, GA distinguishes:
> MBAMBA (ki-)
> MBAKA
> and probably other sub-dialects, but 'linguistic differences . . . are hard to detect except in matters of regional vocabulary'.

†KIMBUNDO of Nambuangongo Post in Ambriz is a mixed language (see KONGO Group, p. 56).
Number: 15,412 (GA, from Census figures).

†MBANGALA (ci-) (see KONGO Group) shows some resemblance to KIMBUNDU and to the CHOKWE-LUNDA Group, p. 67 (GA).

Other names used by various writers include:

SAMA (KISSAMA, QUISSAMA), mentioned by various writers as the name of a MBUNDU tribe, on the coast between R. Cuanza and R. Cuvo, and inland for 60–70 miles.
Number: 8,860 in 1926 (J. Tucker).[1]
BOLO (LIBOLO), south and west of R. Cuanza, south of Malenge and as far as the mid-Cuvo.
SONGO, see SONGU in KONGO and CHOKWE-LUNDA Groups (pp. 56, 67).
NSONGO is mentioned by VBRL, quoting Mendes Correia, as the name of a MBUNDU tribe.
AMBOIM—a place-name; the people are also known as MBUIYI. J. Tucker[2] describes their language as derived from KIMBUNDU and UMBUNDU.
KIBALA (QUIBALA).
LENGUE (QUILENGUE)—obsolete (GA).
NGAGE—obsolete (GA).
DEMBO of Cacuta Caenda.
NGENGU, BONDO, QUEMBO, MUSSENDE.
MAKAMBA (MACAMBA), a name meaning 'friends' in KIMBUNDU; it does not denote any particular tribe or language (GA).

---

[1] *Angola. The Land of the Blacksmith Prince.*   [2] Op. cit.

SAMBA-HOLU GROUP?[1]

Where spoken: C.B., A.

GA	MG3		Other names
SAMBA	SAMBA (u-)	L.12/0	
HOLU (-)			Holo
	(TEMBO	H.34/0)	
? DONGO			

See also KIMBUNDU Group, p. 63.

SAMBA

Where spoken: C.B., between R. Kwango and R. Kwilu just north of the Angola border.
Classed in the LUBA Group by H50 (see p. 72).

HOLU

Where spoken: A., Tembo Aluma, Marimba Post, and in Luremo; probably also across R. Kwango into C.B.
Number: 12,016 (from Census figures).
The HOLU claim relationship with the SAMBA; the name Samba is that of a former Queen, Holu that of her daughter, who succeeded her.
HOLU has affinities with Zone L of MG3 rather than with either KONGO or KIMBUNDU.
MG3's TEMBO (H.34) must be included under HOLU. It is the name of a place called after a former chief.
HOLU is perhaps also spoken by the DONGO (see note under KIMBUNDU, p. 63).

Note: The units composing MG3's Groups H.30 and H.40 have all been placed in other Groups:

H.31 YAKA, see KONGO Group, pp. 57, 58.
H.32 SUKU, see KONGO and CHOKWE-LUNDA Groups, pp. 61, 67.
H.33 HUNGU, see KONGO Group, p. 62.
H.34 TEMBO, see under HOLU.
H.35 MBANGALA, see KONGO, KIMBUNDU, and CHOKWE-LUNDA Groups, pp. 62, 64, 67.
    YONGO, a place-name.
H.36 SHINJI, see KONGO and CHOKWE-LUNDA Groups, pp. 61, 67.
H.41 MBALA, see KONGO Group, p. 60.
H.42 HUDANNA, see KONGO Group, p. 57.

[1] All information on this Group from Atkins, 'A Demographic Survey . . .' and personal communication.

KWANGALI SINGLE UNIT

Where spoken: A., S.W.A., B.P.

EW[1] and Köhler[2]	MG[3]	*Other names*
KWANGALI (si-, ru-) (kwaŋgaṛi)		Kwangari
SAMBYU (ʃi-)		Sambio, Sambiu
MBOGEDU (ʃi-) (/giriku)		Diriku, Diriko, Dirico, Gciriku
MBUKUSHU (θi-)	(MPUKUSHU K.33/o)	Mampukush, Mambukush, Mbukuhu, Goya, Goba

Westphal calls this the 'Okavango dialect group'. These dialects are spoken in the Okavango River Native Territory of S.W.A., across the Okavango river into Angola, and across the Caprivi Strip into B.P. The dialects are listed above from west to east. KWANGALI is also spoken by the MBUNDZA or BUNJA.

[1] Westphal and Kampungu, *Kwangali, An Index of Lexical Types* (1958), and Westphal, personal communication.
[2] Personal communication.

CHOKWE-LUNDA GROUP

Where spoken: C.B., A., N.R.

Classification according to Atkins.[1]

GA	MG3		*Other names*
RUUND (u-)	(LUWUNDA (ci-)	L.53/*	Luunda, N. Lunda, Lunda Muatia(m)vua
COKWE (-)[3]	CIOKWE	K.11/*	Chokwe, Cioko, Djok, Shioko, Tschokwe, Tshiboko, Tshiok, &c.
†NUNGO (mi-)			
See also KONGO Group, p. 56.			
LUIMBI	LUIMBI	K.12:	
	⎧LUIMBI (ci-)	K.12a/*	Luimbe, Lwimbi
	⎨AMBWELA	K.12b/o	
	⎩NGANGWELA	K.12c/o	
	See note below.		
LUCAZI	LUCAZI (ci-)	K.13/*	Luchazi, Lujazi, Ponda
LWENA	LWENA (-)	K.14/*	Luena, Lovale, Lubale, Luvale
MBUNDA	MBUNDA (ci-)	K.15/*	Mbuunda, Gimbunda, Kimbunda
NYENGO	NYENGO	K.16/o	
See also LUYANA Group, p. 70.			
	? MBWELA	K.17/o	Mbwera, Ambuella
	? NKANGALA	K.18/o	
LUNDA	(LUNDA (ci-)	L.52/*	S. Lunda NDƐMBƆ (H50), Ndembu
	(SOLI (ci-)	M.62/*	
	See ILA Group, p. 83.		
†SUKU (ki-)	(SUKU (ki-)	H.32/o	
See also KONGO Group.			
†SHINJI (-)	(SHINJI (-)	H.36/o	Nungo
See also KONGO Group.			
†SONGU (-)	(SONGO	H.26/o	Nsongo
See also KONGO Group and KIMBUNDU, pp. 56, 63.			
†MBANGALA (ci-)			
See also KONGO Group and KIMBUNDU.			

Note: The name NGANGELA (Portuguese GANGUELLA) is a name used by the ovi-Mbundu for the LUIMBI, LUCAZI, MBUNDA, MBWELA, &c.[3] This may be the same as MG3's AMBWELA and NGANGWELA, and may

---

[1] Personal communication.
[2] The prefix **ci-** is probably embedded in the name CIOKWE (ci-OKWE) (GA).
[3] McCulloch, *The Ovimbundu of Angola* (Eth. Survey, 1952).

be connected with MBWELA and perhaps even with NKANGALA. McCulloch[1] refers to 'the Mbwela (or Ambuella) of south-eastern Angola'.

RUUND (u-)

Where spoken: C.B. and A., mainly on the east bank of the upper Lulua, 21°–23° E., 7°–10° S. (GA).

DB points out that this language 'must be rigidly differentiated from Lunda'. GA confirms this statement, and draws attention to the zero suffixes in RUUND.[2] DB, however, classes it in the LUBA Group.

Stappers[3] distinguishes a dialect, spoken by the BEENA TUBEYA, who call themselves KANINKIN, in C.B., Kasaï Prov., on the Katanga Prov. border between R. Mbuyimaji and R. Yabuy.

Number: BEENA TUBEYA c. 20,000 (Stappers).

COKWE

Where spoken: C.B., A., N.R., in a vast area mainly between R. Kwilu and R. Kasaï, from 5° S. southwards through north-western Angola to the Lobito–Katanga railway, extending northwards into Katanga Prov., south-east into north-western Rhodesia, especially Balovale D., south and south-west through Angola, west into ovi-MBUNDU country (McCulloch).[4]

Number: Estimated at over 600,000 (McCulloch).

The language is expanding and absorbing a number of lesser languages (GA). It is used for religious instruction.

†NUNGO (mi-) (see KONGO Group), is described by White[5] as almost indistinguishable from COKWE.

LUIMBI (ci-)

Where spoken: A., east of the upper Cuango and Cuilo rivers, 11° 20'–15° S., and eastwards to the upper Kweio and Lungé Bungo rivers.

Number: A few hundreds (McCulloch).

McCulloch gives MBANDE as a name for either the southern LUIMBI or a closely related people.

LUCAZI (ci-)

Where spoken: A., N.R. (a) between Cuando swamp and the upper Lungé Bungo, 19° 30'–21° 10' E.; (b) in a small enclave round and slightly north-east of the Dongwa-Kabompo swamp.

Number: c. 60,000 (White).

LWENA

Where spoken: A., N.R., on the upper Zambezi, 11°–14° 30' S., in an area bounded in the south-west by the lower Lungé Bungo, but extending for about 100 miles each way.

---

[1] *The Southern Lunda and Related Peoples*.   [2] See MG1, p. 56.
[3] 'Een Ruund dialekt: de taal der Beena Tubeya' (*Kongo-Overzee*, 1954).
[4] *The Southern Lunda*. . . .   [5] Quoted in McCulloch, op. cit.

CHOKWE-LUNDA GROUP 69

Number: N.R. 68,443 (1934 Census); estimated by White at 90,000.

LWENA is accepted as one of the main languages of N.R., used a medium of primary education, and studied as a subject throughout the school course. It is used as a lingua franca by speakers of related languages.

MBUNDA (ci-)

Where spoken: A., N.R. (*a*) between 13° and 15° S., between the Lumai–Ciume road in the west and 22° E. in the east, and in a narrow belt extending to the Zambezi in the south-east; to the north, between R. Lungé Bungo and R. Luanginga; (*b*) on the west bank of the Zambezi just below the Lueti confluence; (*c*) in a small enclave about 15° 20′ S., 23° 50′ E.; (*d*) in a small enclave about 14° 20′ S., 23° 40′ E.

Number: N.R. 23,673 (1934 Census).

NYENGO

Where spoken: A., N.R., in a small area on R. Luangwa.
Number: N.R. 4,457 (1934 Census).
According to Gluckman[1] the NYENGO speak KOLOLO (i.e. LOZI) (see pp. 71, 151).

MBWELA

Where spoken: A., between R. Cuando and R. Cubango.

The MBWELA are probably related to the MBWERA or MBWELA of N.R. (see p. 75), but 'they have been separated for several centuries and are now separate both linguistically and culturally' (McCulloch).[2]

NKANGALA

Where spoken: A., between 15° S. and the Cuando swamp, 21° 30′–21° 50′ E.

LUNDA (ci-)

Where spoken: C.B., A., N.R., in a vast area including a large part of the upper basins of R. Lulua and R. Kasaï, from Liuwa plain in the south to 7° 30′ S.; an extensive belt westwards to the upper Kwango; in the south-east a belt extends from the headwaters of R. Zambezi, R. Lubudi, and R. Kabompo to 14° S.

Number: N.R. 82,044 (1934 Census).

H50 names a dialect:
NDƐMBƆ, spoken in C.B., extending into N.R. NDEMBU is referred to by McCulloch[3] as 'the Lunda dialect reduced to writing'.

LUNDA is used by Protestant missions, at least in C.B.

SOLI (ci-), placed by MG3 in the ILA Group (see p. 83) is grouped here by DB.

According to GA the following dialects stand between the KONGO and CHOKWE-LUNDA Groups:
†SHINJI, SUKU, SONGU, MBANGALA.

[1] Quoted in Turner, *The Lozi Peoples of North-Western Rhodesia* (Eth. Survey, 1952).
[2] Op. cit.   [3] Op. cit.

LUYANA GROUP

Where spoken: N.R. (and A.)

MG3		Gluckman[1]	Other names
LUYANA (esi-)	K.31/*	LUYI	Lui, Luiana, Luano, Louyi, Rouyi; YANA (lu-)[2]
		KWANDI	
MBOWE (esi-)	K.32/*	(MBOWE, see below)	
MPUKUSHU	K.33/o		
But see KWANGALI, p. 66.			
		LOZI tribes:	
†(LOZI (si-)	K.21/*)	⎧LOZI	Kololo, Rozi, Rotse, Rozvi
See also SOTHO Group, p. 148.		⎪MBOWE	
		⎨KWANDI (but see under LUYI above)	
KWANGWA	K.37/o	⎪KWANGWA	
		⎩MWENYI	Muenyi
		LOZI-ized tribes:	
		⎧NYENGO	
		⎪ See also CHOKWE-LUNDA Group, p. 67.	
		⎪MAKOMA	
		⎪NDUNDULU	Imilangu
SIMAA	K.35/o	⎨SIMAA	
MASHI	K.34/o	⎪MASHI	
SHANJO	K.36/o	⎪SHANJO	
		⎪MISHULUNDU	
		⎪YEI	
		⎩MBUNDA	

Of this Group, MG1 says, 'the data are altogether inadequate'.

LUYI or LUYANA is the language originally spoken by the LUYI, LUIZI, or LOZI, and which still appears to be spoken by some people, though it has been largely superseded by LOZI. It is classed as a separate language within the Group by MG3, but is not shown on the map in MG1.

Number: 3,285 LUANO.[3]

According to Gluckman a LUYI dialect is spoken by:

KWANDI, on R. Lui just above its confluence with the Zambezi.

Number: 2,510.

MBOWE (esi-)

Where spoken: Between R. Zambezi and R. Kabompo at their confluence.
Number: 5,336.

Classed by MG3 as a separate language; Gluckman lists MBOWE among the LOZI tribes.

[1] *Economy of the Central Barotse Plain* (Rhodes-Livingstone Papers, 7, 1941).
[2] Atkins, personal communication. [3] N.R. figures for this Group from 1934 Census.

LUYANA GROUP

MPUKUSHU is classed in this Group by MG3. But see KWANGARI, p. 66.

The other names given by MG3 as those of units in the LUYANA Group are given by Gluckman as those of LOZI-speaking tribes.

LOZI (si-) (KOLOLO) is spoken by LOZI and related tribes, and by several tribes of non-LOZI origin, now LOZI-ized.

The KOLOLO conquerors of the LOZI in the nineteenth century spoke SOTHO and the present LOZI language is a mixture of SOTHO and LUYI. It is described by Westphal[1] as having a largely non-SOTHO grammar and about 50 per cent. SOTHO vocabulary; according to DSB it is an offshoot of SOTHO considerably influenced by Central Bantu, particularly LUYI.

Its use has been fostered by missions and it is now the lingua franca of Barotseland and one of the four official languages of N.R.

Gluckman lists the following LOZI tribes:

The 'LUYANA' Group:

LOZI, in the central Barotse plain.
  Number: 67,193.
MBOWE (see above).
KWANDI (see above, under LUYI).
KWANGWA, in the bend of R. Lui, south-west of R. Luampa.
  Number: 25,497.
MWENYI, on R. Luanginga just above its confluence with the Zambezi.
  Number: 4,018.
Assimilated tribes (LOZI-speaking):
NYENGO. Placed by MG3 in the CHOKWE-LUNDA Group (see p. 67).
MAKOMA, on R. Luanginga adjacent to the NYENGO.
  Number: 7,605.
NDUNDULU, on the Angola border, north of the SIMAA.
  Number: 21,962.
SIMAA, between R. Kwando and R. Lueti.
  Number: 9,109.
MASHI, on R. Kwando south of the SIMAA.
  Number: 4,500.
SHANJO, between R. Zambezi and R. Kwando just north of the Caprivi Strip.
  Number: 7,910.
MISHULUNDU (no location or figures given).
YEI (no location or figures given).
MBUNDA[2] immigrants, now completely assimilated, scattered mainly along the right bank of the Zambezi.

---
[1] Personal communication.   [2] See CHOKWE-LUNDA Group, p. 67.

LUBA GROUP[1]

Where spoken: C.B. (and N.R.).

MG3		Other names
KETE (lu-)	L.21/o	Kikete
BINJI	L.22/o	Bindji
SONGE (lu-)	L.23/*	SƆNGƐ (ki-) (H50), Songi, Kalebwe, NE. Luba, Yembe
		MBALA (ru-) (VBRL)
		LWALU (VBRL)
(BANGOBANGO	D.27/o)	Bangubangu
See LEGA Group, p. 92.		
(SALAMPASU	L.51/*)	sala-MPASU (tʃi-) (VBRL)
		LUNTU (VBRL)
LUNA	L.24/*	Luna Inkongo, N. Luba
LUBA-LULUA	L.30:	Kalebwe, W. Luba, Tshiluba, Luva
⎧ LUBA (ci-), Kasaï	L.31a/*	
⎨ LULUA	L.31b/*	
⎩ LANGE (ciʃi-)	L.31c/o	
KANYOKA (ci-)	L.32/*	KANYƆKA (H50), Kanioka
LUBA (ki-), Katanga	L.33/*	LUBA (Burssens)
HEMBA (ki-)	L.34/*	LUBA-HƐMBA (H50), E. Luba
†SANGA	L.35/*	Chiluba, Luba-Sanga, S. Luba
See also BEMBA Group, p. 80.		
SAMBA (u-)	L.12/o)	Shankadi
But see SAMBA-HOLU Group, p. 65.		
†(KAONDE (ki-)	L.41/*)	Kahonde, Kawonde
See also BEMBA Group.		
(MBWERA (ʃi-)	L.61/o)	
See NKOYA Group, p. 75.		

VBRL gives a list of names under 'LUBA', which, however, according to Vansina[3] are those of KUBA tribes. See KUBA Group, p. 54.

KETE (lu-)

Where spoken: (*a*) in a small area north-west of Lusambo on R. Sankuru around Bena Dibele; (*b*) in a small area south and east of the Luba–Lulua confluence, around Bena Makima and as far as 5° S.; (*c*) in a narrow strip between R. Lulua and R. Bushimaie south of Dibaya; (*d*) in a small enclave, 5° 40′ S., 24° E.

Classed by DB as a LUBA dialect.

BINJI

Where spoken: Round Lualabourg on both banks of R. Lulua, eastwards and southwards to R. Kasaï on the Angola border.

[1] Comprising Groups L.20 and L.30 of MG3.
[2] *Les Tribus Bakuba et les peuplades apparentées.*

LUBA GROUP

Number: 64,000 (VBRL).

VBRL refers twice[1] to BINDJI (i) as a 'substrat' language, attached to LUBA; (ii) grouped with KETE (two dialectal variants).

SONGE (lu-)

Where spoken: In a roughly triangular area with base on 5° S., between R. Lualaba and R. Sankuru.

According to H50 ki-SƆNGƐ of the upper Lomami is a LUBA dialect which has often been classed as a separate language.

SONGE is used as a medium of communication among tribes in Terr. Kabinda, where it is known as 'ki-SONGE universel'.[2]

VBRL adds:
MBALA, on R. Lweta. No linguistic information available.

LWALU (20,700).

sala-MPASU (tʃi-) (60,000).

The speech of the bakwa-LUNTU (100,000).

BANGUBANGU

Where spoken: In Maniema Prov., Terr. Kabambare.
Classed by Meeussen[3] in the LUBA Group, and described as having affinities with SONGE. But see also LEGA Group, p. 92.

LUNA

Where spoken: In a small area around Lusambo and to the south.

LUBA-LULUA:

LUBA (ci-) of Kasaï.

Where spoken: North of a line from Tshekapa to Dimbelenge.

LULUA

Where spoken: In the same area as LUBA of Kasaï.
Described by H50 as considerably divergent from LUBA; by VBRL as a 'substrat' language.

LANGE (ciʃi-)

Where spoken: South of LUBA of Kasaï and LULUA.

According to H50 LUBA is spoken by a number of tribes which have been at some time subjected to the LUBA, or have adopted the language spontaneously; it is also spoken as a second language by the KUBA and the ba-MBAGANI.

LUBA is used in sub-standard education and religious instruction.

[1] pp. 399, 505.   [2] Samain, 'Les Basonge' (*Congo*, 1924).
[3] *Linguistische Schets van het Bangubangu*, 1954; 'De talen van Maniema (Belgisch Kongo)', 1953.

LUBA GROUP

KANYOKA

Where spoken: Between R. Bushimaie and R. Luembe at 7° S., and farther south. Described by H50 as a LUBA dialect, by VBRL as a 'substrat' language.

LUBA (ki-) of Katanga

Where spoken: Over a wide area mainly west of R. Lualaba, between 5° and 10° S., bounded in the west by R. Lomami in the northern part of the area, extending westwards to Luembe and Lusiloshi, eastwards to R. Lualaba in the Kibara mountains area.

HEMBA (ki-)

Where spoken: In an area about 250 miles from north to south, mainly east of R. Lualaba on both banks of R. Luva, northwards to just beyond R. Lukuga, southwestwards to L. Mweru, eastwards to within 30 miles of the Tanganyika border.

Considered as a LUBA dialect by both H50 and VBRL.

†SANGA

Where spoken: In an area about 30 miles east of the upper Lualaba, 10°–11° S., 26° 20'–27° 20' E.

H50 describes it as a LUBA dialect forming a transition between LUBA and BEMBA; according to VBRL it is a 'substrat' language much influenced by LUBA-HEMBA.

SAMBA is classed as a LUBA dialect by H50. But see SAMBA-HOLU Group, p. 65.

VBRL adds to this Group:

The speech of the ba-ZELA (of which, however, nothing is known).

†KAONDE (ci-)

Where spoken: C.B. and N.R., south and west from the headwaters of R. Lualaba, between 10° and 15° S., westwards to R. Kabongo and R. Luampa, eastwards to R. Lushwishi, southwards a little beyond R. Kafue at 15° S.

Number: N.R. 37,952 (1934 Census).

According to DB a LUBA dialect; according to VBRL either akin to BEMBA or a 'substrat' language. See also BEMBA Group, p. 80.

MBWERA (ʃi-) is described by van Eeden[1] as closely related to LUBA. But see NKOYA Group, p. 75.

[1] 'Notes on Soli grammar' (*Z.E.S.*, 1926).

(75)

NKOYA GROUP

Where spoken: N.R.

	MG3	McCulloch (Tribes)[1]
NKOYA (ʃi-)	L.62/*	NKOYA
MBWERA (ʃi-)	L.61/o	MBWELA
		LUKOLWE
		MASHASHA
		LUSHANGE

McCulloch states that: 'The various groups of Nkoya–Mbwela peoples ... are known to form a distinct group linguistically.' They are grouped by DB with LUBA and northern LUNDA. The classification of MG3 is followed here.

NKOYA (ʃi-)

Where spoken: (*a*) In central Mankoya D., between R. Luampa and R. Luafuta; (*b*) in north-west Mankoya D. and north-east Mongu D.; (*c*) in Kalabo D. west of R. Zambezi; (*d*) in Nalalo D. on the right bank of the upper Lumbe; (*e*) on the northern boundaries of Livingstone and Kalomo Districts (these people are sometimes known as SHIKALU).

Number: 18,543.[2]

According to McCulloch 'more or less distinct dialects' are spoken in these five areas.

MBWERA (ʃi-)

Where spoken: In the R. Dongwe area of north Mankoya D.; around the Kabompo–Dongwe confluence and upstream on the right bank of the Kabompo; also scattered farther north and east.

It is not clear whether LUKOLWE is an alternative name for the MBWERA or that of a separate tribe in the same area.

Number: MBWELA 4,052, LUKOLWE 9,351.

See also LUBA Group, p. 72.

The MBWERA are related to the MBWELA of Angola, but their languages appear to be no longer related (see MBWELA, p. 69).

Two other tribes are included by McCulloch in the NKOYA–MBWELA peoples: MASHASHA, in southern Mankoya D., extending into Mumbwa D., near R. Lunga.

Number: 13,083.

LUSHANGE, in Mankoya D., on R. Luena.

Number: 9,349.

[1] *The Southern Lunda and Related Peoples.*   [2] Figures for this Group from 1934 Census.

FIPA-MAMBWE GROUP

Where spoken: T.T., N.R.

MG3		*Other names*
PIMBWE (ici-)	M.11/*	
RUNGWA (ici-)	M.12/o	
FIPA (ici-)	M.13/*	
RUNGU (ici-)	M.14/*	Lungu
MAMBWE (ici-)	M.15/*	Kimambwe

FIPA, RUNGU, and MAMBWE are classed with BEMBA (see p. 80) by DB.

PIMBWE (ici-)

Where spoken: T.T., in the neighbourhood of Mpimbwe north-west of L. Rukwa.
Number: 7,881.[1]

RUNGWA (ici-)

Where spoken: T.T., north-west of L. Rukwa between R. Kavu in the south-west, 7° S. in the north and 32° E. in the east.
Number: 4,551.

FIPA (ici-)

Where spoken: T.T., on the eastern shore of L. Tanganyika, 7°–8° S., eastwards nearly to Mpimbwe in the northern part of the area, southwards nearly to L. Rukwa.
Number: 78,252.
Classed in the BEMBA Group by DB.

RUNGU (ici-)

Where spoken: T.T. and N.R., at the southern end of L. Tanganyika, in an area including Mpulungu, Kituta, and Abercorn.
Number: T.T. 9,617, N.R. 24,028.
Classed as a BEMBA dialect by DB.

MAMBWE (ici-)

Where spoken: T.T. and N.R., 8°–9° 30′ S., 31° 30′–32° E., as far as L. Rukwa in the north-east.
Number: T.T. 13,311, N.R. 14,886.

Note: A 'Union version', called MAMBWE-LUNGU, has been used for translation of the New Testament.

[1] Figures for this Group from 1948 Census (T.T.) and 1934 Census (N.R.).

NYIHA-SAFWA GROUP

Where spoken: T.T., N.R., N.

MG3		*Other names*
WANDA (ici-)	M.21/*	Wandia
		NDALI
MWANGA (iciina-)	M.22/*	Namwanga, Nyamwanga, Inamwanga
NYIHA (iʃi-)	M.23/*	Nyika, Nyixa
MALILA (iʃi-)	M.24/*	
SAFWA (iʃi-)	M.25/*	
IWA	M.26/o	
TAMBO	M.27/o	Tembo
See also TUMBUKA, p. 137.		
(LAMBIA	N.21/o)	LAMBYA (ici-), Lambwa
See also TUMBUKA.		

WANDA (ici-)

Where spoken: T.T., south of L. Rukwa, 8° 30′ S., 32° 20′ E.
Number: 6,303.[1]

NDALI

Where spoken: T.T., west of the northern end of L. Nyasa between R. Kibila and R. Songwe.[2]
Number: 50,799.
NDALI occurs in the Index to MG1, with reference number M.21 (see WANDA above), but is not mentioned in the text.

MWANGA (iciina-)

Where spoken: T.T. and N.R., in an area centred on Mwenzo, about 40 miles on each side of the boundary.
Number: T.T. 22,663, N.R. 8,965.
Tew[3] groups NYAMWANGA ethnically with NYAKYUSA (see p. 79), but makes no statement about language.

NYIHA (iʃi-)

Where spoken: T.T. and N.R., a little to the south of L. Rukwa, 9° 5′ S., 33° E.
Number: T.T. 58,747.

MALILA (iʃi-)

Where spoken: T.T., just north of the N.R. border, about 30° E.
Number: 17,426.

[1] Figures for this Group from 1948 Census (T.T.) and 1934 Census (N.R.).
[2] Berger, 'Ndali-Texte' (*Z.E.S.*, 1935).
[3] *Peoples of the Lake Nyasa Region* (Eth. Survey, 1950).

NYIHA-SAFWA GROUP

SAFWA (iʃi-)

Where spoken: T.T., between L. Rukwa and L. Nyasa around Mbeya, eastwards to Magoje, northwards almost to 8° S.
Number: 46,289.

IWA

Where spoken: N.R., in a narrow belt south of the T.T. border, near the Nyasaland border, on the Chambezi–Luangwa sources watershed.
Number: 6,863.
Tew[1] groups IWA with NYAKYUSA, but gives no linguistic information.

TAMBO

Where spoken: N.R., south-west of the N. border around the source of R. Luangwa.
Number: 3,264.

LAMBYA (ici-)

Where spoken: T.T. and N., on both banks of R. Songwe.
Number: T.T. 7,467.
According to Tew[2] the LAMBYA are said to be culturally related to the NYAKYUSA. Busse[3] describes their language as a mixed language, related to TUMBUKA, much influenced by NDALI. J. Kalinga, himself a mu-LAMBYA, states that his language is interintelligible with NYIHA, which he considers to be more closely related than any Nyasaland language.[4]

[1] Op. cit.
[3] 'Lambya-Texte' (*Z.E.S.*, 1940)
[2] Op. cit.
Personal communication.

NYAKYUSA SINGLE UNIT[1]

Where spoken: T.T., N.R., N.

MG3	Tew (Tribes)[2]	Other names
NYEKYOSA (eke-) M.31/*	NYAKYUSA:	Mombe (old name)
	NYAKYUSA	Niakiusa, Nyakusa, Nyikyusa, Sokile, Sokili, Sochile
	KUKWE	
	SELYA	Salya, Seria
	MWAMBA	Lungulu
	NGONDE	Konde, Nkonde
	KINGA	

But see KINGA in HEHE Group, p. 131.
NYAMWANGA ⎫ see NYIHA-SAFWA Group,
IWA   ⎬ p. 77.

NYEKYOSA (eke-)

Where spoken: T.T., Rungwe D., also in Mbeya D., on the northern shores of L. Nyasa, on the western shore as far as R. Songwe and on the eastern shore as far as the Livingstone mountains.

In Nyasaland the language is known as NGONDE,[3] and is spoken in the plain on the western shore of L. Nyasa, between R. Rkukuru and R. Songwe.

Number: T.T. 191,901 (1948 Census), N. 62,136.

Tew adds to the NYAKYUSA tribes:

KINGA, in T.T., in the Livingstone mountains on the eastern shore of L. Nyasa in Njombe D.

Perhaps, however, these are the KINGA whose speech is classed by MG3 in the HEHE Group (p. 131).

---

[1] Called KONDE Group in MG3. The name used here is that most widely known, in the spelling most frequently used in literature.

[2] *Peoples of the Lake Nyasa Region*.

[3] Tew, quoting Godfrey Wilson, says: 'In language as well as culture, the Ngonde of Nyasaland are identical with the Nyakyusa of Tanganyika.'

BEMBA GROUP[1]

Where spoken: C.B., N.R.

MG3		DB[2]		Other names
(TAABWA (ici-)	M.41/*	TABWA	(a)	Rungu
SHILA	M.41/o			
				BWILE, Bwile, Bwila, Bile
BEMBA	M.42:	BEMBA	(a)	Wemba
(BEMBA (ici-)	M.42/*			
NGOMA[3]	M.42/o			
LOMOTUA	M.42/o			Lomotwa, Lɔmɔtwa
NWESI	M.42/o			
LEMBUE	M.42/o			
(MAMBWE	M.15/*)	MAMBWE	(a)	
See FIPA-MAMBWE Group, p. 76.				
(RUNGU	M.14/*)	LUNGU	(a)	
See FIPA-MAMBWE Group.				
		AUSHI	(b)	Ushi, Usi, Uzhil
BIISA (ici-)	M.51/*	BISA	(d)	Wisa
LALA (ici-)	M.52/*	LALA	(e)	
		AMBO		
SWAKA (ici-)	M.53/*	MASWAKA	(e)	
LAMBA (ici-)	M.54/*	LAMBA	(c)	
SEBA	M.55/o	SEŴA	(c)	Sewa, Shishi
		ŴULIMA	(c)	
		LUANO	(c)	
(MWANGA (iciina-)	M.22/*)	NAMWANGA	(f)	
See NYIHA-SAFWA Group, p. 77.				
(FIPA	M.13/*)	FIPA	(g)	
See FIPA-MAMBWE Group.				
†(SANGA	L.35/*)			
See also LUBA Group, p. 72.				
†(KAONDE	L.41/*)			
See also LUBA Group.				

TAABWA (ici-)

Where spoken: C.B., N.R., between 7° and 9° 30′ S., from the eastern slopes of the Mujila mountains to L. Tanganyika, southwards beyond the southern tip of the lake, westwards beyond L. Mweru.

In MG1 two dialects are distinguished:

[1] The BEMBA and BISA-LALA Groups of MG3 combined.
[2] Letters in brackets refer to sub-groupings within the BEMBA Group.
[3] Dialects listed in MG1.

BEMBA GROUP

TAABWA, spoken in the main part of the area.
Number: N.R. 7,918.[1]
SHILA, on the southern and eastern shores of L. Mweru; shown on Whiteley's map west of L. Mweru.[2]
TAABWA is also spoken by the BWILE north of L. Mweru.
Number: 4,745.

BEMBA (ici-)

Where spoken: N.R., in a vast area between 9° and 12° S., 29° and 32° E.; also in C.B. (spoken by minorities living in reserves).
Number: N.R. *c.* 140,000 (A. Richards),[3] C.B. *c.* 30,000 in 1937.[4]

BEMBA is the lingua franca of the Copperbelt, and the official language of a large part of N.R. It is used in primary education in the whole of the BEMBA-speaking area, and also in the northern part of N.R. In C.B. it is mainly spoken by a minority in Elisabethville (but ki-NGWANA is also used).

The Bible has been translated, and there is an increasing amount of vernacular literature. The Bible in a 'Union' version is in preparation.

In MG1 the following dialects are distinguished:

BEMBA
NGOMA, spoken on the west bank of R. Luapula, between 10° and 11° S.
LOMOTUA, spoken by a few people in C.B., in the Kundelungu mountains.
NWESI, in a small pocket in the north-eastern part of the BEMBA area.
LEMBUE, in the north-eastern part of the area.

To these DB adds TABWA (see above), MAMBWE and LUNGU (see FIPA-MAMBWE Group, p. 76).

AUSHI, spoken along R. Luapula and into C.B., is classed as a BEMBA dialect by H50.
Number: N.R. 28,958.

BIISA (ici-)

Where spoken: N.R., on the slopes of the Machinga mountains and mainly on the west bank of R. Luangwa, 13°–13° 30′ S., and in a belt to the north-west, including part of the Bangweulu (Bangweolo) swamps.
Number: 41,591.

LALA (ici-)

Where spoken: N.R., C.B., in the 'neck' of N.R. from just west of the C.B. border to R. Luangwa, and northwards to L. Bangweulu.
Number: (estimated) N.R. 50,000, C.B. 10,000 (Lambo).[5]

---

[1] Figures from 1934 Census, unless otherwise stated.
[2] *Bemba and Related Peoples of Northern Rhodesia* (Eth. Survey, 1951).
[3] *Land, Labour and Diet in Northern Rhodesia* (1939).
[4] Whiteley, op. cit.
[5] 'Étude sur les Balala' (*Bull. Jur. indig.*, 1946).

BEMBA GROUP

AMBO[1]

Where spoken: Mainly in the middle and lower valley of R. Lukushashi and its tributaries.

Number: (estimated) 11,000+.

Spoken by a LALA offshoot calling themselves BAMBO or KAMBONSENGA. Their speech 'hardly deserves to be classified as a separate language, but may be designated a dialect of LALA'. It contains many NSENGA words (see p. 141).

According to Whiteley[2] LUANO should be classed with LALA. DB groups it with LAMBA (see below).

SWAKA (ici-)

Where spoken: N.R., C.B., from the southern bend of R. Luapula across a narrow strip of C.B. territory to Chibwe.

Number: N.R. 12,496.

Grouped with LALA by DB, with LAMBA by Whiteley.

LAMBA (ici-)

Where spoken: N.R., C.B., north of Lukanga swamp on both banks of R. Kafue and R. Lushwishi, extending in the north-east almost to R. Luapula; also farther north, in the Elisabethville area.

Number: N.R. c. 20,000 (Whiteley);[3] total 70,000–80,000 (Doke).[4]

SEBA

Where spoken: C.B., N.R., in the Elisabethville area and for about 70 miles to the south, 50 miles east, 50 miles west.

Number: C.B. 4,000+, N.R. 3,137.

Classed as a LAMBA dialect by DB, who also adds:

WULIMA

LUANO, in the area of R. Mulungushi and R. Lunsefwa.

Number: 3,285.

Grouped with LALA by Whiteley (see above).

FIPA and NAMWANGA are also included in the BEMBA Group by DB. But see FIPA-MAMBWE and NYIHA-SAFWA Groups, pp. 76, 77.

†H50 suggests affinities of SANGA and KAONDE (see LUBA Group, p. 72) with BEMBA.

---

[1] Whiteley, op. cit.   [2] Op. cit.
[3] Op. cit.   [4] *Textbook of Lamba Grammar* (1938).

ILA GROUP[1]

Where spoken: N.R., S.R.

MG3		Jaspan[2]	Other names
LENJE (ci-)	M.61/*		Ciina Mukuni
			TWA (DB, VBRL)
SOLI (ci-)	M.62/*		
See also CHOKWE-LUNDA Group, p. 67.			
ILA (ci-)	M.63/*		Sukulumbwe, Shukulumbwe
TONGA	M.64:	TONGA:	
⎧TONGA (ci-)	M.64/*	⎧Plateau TONGA	
⎨TOKA	M.64/o	⎨S. TONGA	
⎪		⎪Valley TONGA	We
⎩LEYA	M.64/o	⎩LEYA	
(TOTELA (eci-)	K.41/*)	TOTELA	
See TOTELA Group, p. 85.			
(SU̱BIYA (eci-)	K.42/*)	SUBIYA	Ikuhane
See TOTELA Group.			
			LUNDWE (VBRL)
			MALA (VBRL)

LENJE (ci-)

Where spoken: N.R., in the Lukanga swamp area north of Lusaka, 27° 30'–29° E., and southwards to R. Kafue.
Number: 32,679 in 1946 (Jaspan).
DB and VBRL add the little-known dialect:
TWA, spoken in the swamps of R. Kafue and R. Lukanga.

SOLI (ci-)

Where spoken: N.R., in two reserves in Lusaka D.
Number: c. 13,000 in 1946 (Jaspan).
Classed with LUNDA by DB (see p. 67).

ILA (ci-)

Where spoken: N.R., on both banks of R. Kafue, 26°–27° E., northwards to 15° S., south to 16° 30' S.
Number: c. 13,000 (Jaspan).

TONGA (ci-)

Where spoken: N.R., S.R., mainly on the north bank of the middle Zàmbezi between 25° and 29° E., north to R. Kafue at Nega-Nega and to the Kafue–Zambezi confluence; also south of the Zambezi in a triangular area between R. Sanyati and R. Sangani.

---

[1] Called LENJE-TONGA Group in MG3. The name used here is that of the best-known unit in the Group.   [2] *The Ila-Tonga Peoples of North-Western Rhodesia* (Eth. Survey, 1953).

ILA GROUP

Number: Estimated 70,000–110,000 (Jaspan).
TONGA dialects:
  'Plateau TONGA', the prevalent dialect;
  S. TONGA (TOKA);
  'Valley TONGA' (WE), in the Gwembe (lower Zambezi) valley.
With the TONGA dialects are also classed:
  LEYA, in the south-eastern corner of Livingstone D.;
  TOTELA and SUBIYA (see below);
and, according to VBRL:
  LUNDWE and MALA.

Authorities differ as to the classification of TOTELA and SUBIYA. In the Ethnographic Survey TOTELA is classed with TONGA; DB groups it with TONGA; Gluckman[1] substantiates this classification; VBRL quotes Torrend as classing TOTELA as a subdivision of TONGA. SUBIYA is classed with TONGA in the Ethnographic Survey, and described as closely related to ILA; DB groups LUYI (see LUYANA Group, p. 70), LEYA and SUBIYA under the heading 'Zambezi group (allied to Tonga)', and VBRL's classification tallies with this. On the other hand, MG3 considers TOTELA and SUBIYA to constitute a separate Group in Zone K.

[1] Quoted in Jaspan, op. cit.

TOTELA GROUP?[1]

Where spoken: N.R.

MG3		*Other names*
TOTELA (eci-)	K.41/*	
SU̱BIYA (eci-)	K.42/*	IKUHANE (ci-) (Westphal);[2] Subiya, Subia, Subya. Soubiya, Ikwahani

TOTELA (eci-)

Where spoken: Between R. Njoko and R. Zambezi.
Number: 14,160 (1934 Census).

IKUHANE (ci-) (SU̱BIYA)

Where spoken: (*a*) South of R. Linyanti and R. Zambezi, 24°–26° 30' S., to 19° E.; (*b*) in a belt about 10 miles wide on the north bank of R. Zambezi, 24° 30'–25° 10' S.
Number: 2,950 (1934 Census).

Both these languages have been classed in the ILA Group by several authorities (see p. 83).

[1] Called SUBIYA Group in MG3. The name TOTELA has been used here, as SUBIYA does not seem to be the true name of the language. [2] Personal communication.

KARI GROUP

Where spoken: C.B., O.-C., Sudan.

NBii			Other names
li-KARI-li	Extr. N., A	1	Kare
NYANGA-li		2a	
GBATI-ri		2b	Gbote
MAYEKA		2d[1]	
li-NGBEE		3	Lingbe, Mangbele
HOMA	Extr. N., B	1a	
BODO		1b	Bɔdɔ
BOGURU:		1c	
('BA)BUKUR		1	
KOGORO		2	Boguru, Bukuru, Guru
BOGURU		3	
NGBINDA (bu-)		2	

These languages are divided in NBii into:
  A. Those having vestigial suffixes.
  B. Those having prefixes but no suffixes.

A. Those having vestigial suffixes:

li-KARI-li

Where spoken: C.B., Terr. Ango, Sasa chefferie; O.-C., north of Zemio between R. Chinko and R. Ouarra, along R. Mbomu as far as Karre, in two areas separated by the BIRI (non-Bantu-speaking).

Number: C.B. 1,000, but only the old people now speak the language, the rest having adopted ZANDE; O.-C. 3,000–4,000.[2]

Languages or dialects spoken by the 'pseudo-BANGBA':

NYANGA-li

Where spoken: C.B., Terr. Watsa, in a small enclave (10 villages) among the non-Bantu MAMVU.
Number: 2,130 in 1931.

GBATI-ri

Where spoken: C.B., east of the NYANGA.
Number: 821 in 1931. 'Only a few survivors' still speak this language.
It closely resembles NYANGA-li.

The speech of the MAYEKA (location unknown).

The MABADI now speak MANGBETU (non-Bantu) only. It is not even certain that they ever had a language of their own.

---

[1] The remaining member of this Cluster is given in NBii as MABADI (but see below).
[2] Figures for this Group from NBii.

KARI GROUP

li-NGBEE, spoken by the NGBEE (MANGBELE).

Where spoken: C.B. (*a*) in Terr. Niangara; (*b*) at Gombari.
Number: (*a*) A few elders; (*b*) *c*. 30.

This language was still in existence at Gombari a few years ago, but now MA-NGBETU or MAYOGO is spoken.[1]

B. Those having prefixes but no suffixes:

HOMA

Where spoken: Sudan, around Mopoi and Tambura.
Number: Few.

BODO

Where spoken: Sudan, in the neighbourhood of Dem Zubeir; also said to be in O.-C., in the R. Warra–R. Kerre area.[2]
Number: Few.

BOGURU, comprising:

the speech of the 'BABUKUR
Where spoken: Sudan, west of Yambio.
Number: A few old men only.

KOGORO, spoken by the BABOGORO
Where spoken: O.-C., Bangassou (still in use a generation ago); still spoken amongst expatriates in the north-eastern part of C.B.
Number: Few.

BOGURU, spoken by the BAGBELE
Where spoken: C.B., in two villages north of Garamba National Park.
Number: *c*. 75.

NGBINDA (bu-), spoken by the 'BANGBINDA

Where spoken: Sudan and C.B., in a few scattered spots in the Uele region, and at Kotele village 20 km. from Buta.
Number: Few.

---

[1] See Tucker and Bryan, *The Non-Bantu Languages of North-Eastern Africa*, pp. 8, 23.
[2] See Santandrea, 'Little-known Tribes of the Bahr el Ghazal Basin' (*Sudan Notes*, 1948).

BALI GROUP

Where spoken: C.B.

	NBii		MG3	
LIKO (li-)	Extr. N. Trans. 1			
BAALI (li-):	2	BALI̧	D.21/o	
⎧ 'BAKUNDUMU	a			
⎪ BEKENI	b			
⎨ BEMILI	c			
⎩ BAFWA NDAKA	d			

LIKO (li-), spoken by TORIKO

Where spoken: Terr. Wamba, near Babondei.
Number: 25,962 (NBii).
Also spoken by a group of MABITI (often erroneously classed as MANGBETU) in Terr. Paulis, Gwatala chefferie.
The so-called MALIKO, however, have now largely adopted BUDU (see NYALI Group, p. 101).

BAALI (li-)

Where spoken: Terr. Bafwasende, south of the middle Aruwimi around Panga, as far as R. Tshopo.
Number: 37,738 (NBii).
Four dialects may be distinguished, spoken by:
  'BAKUNDUMU, in the north-east;
  BEKENI, in the west;
  BEMILI;
  BAFWA NDAKA.
BAALI is considerably influenced by BWA (see p. 44). It is used in sub-standard education.
MG considers it as Sub-Bantu, on the basis of manuscript material by Kerrigan.

BIRA GROUP (Sub-Bantu)

Where spoken: C.B., U.

	NBii	NBiii	MG3	Other names
MBUTI (i-)	E., I			MBUTI (ki- or ku-);[1] Kimbuti
KAIKU (i-)	II			
BILA (ki-) (forest)	III			BILA (ku̧-bi̧ṛa)[2]
KUUMU (ki-)	IV	KO̧MO̧	D.23/0	KUMU;[3] Komo
BILI (i-)	V:	PȨRI̧	D.31/*	Pere, Pili, Pakombe
⎧ BILI (i-)	1			
⎪ LEEDJI (e-)	2			
⎨ TIKE (e-)	3			
⎪ BAIDUMBA	4			
⎪ BEKA	5			
⎩ HOKOHOKO	6			
BUGOMBE (e-)	VI			
BIRA (Western)	VII			Babeda, Babera, Babila, Babira
⎧ LENGOLA (ki-)	VIII	LƐNGƆLA	D.12/0	
⎩ MITUKU (kinya-)		MI̧TU̧KU̧	D.13/0	

See also LEGA and MBOLE-ENA Groups, pp. 92, 103.

BIRA (ki-) (plains)	IX			
BIRA (ki-) (Ruwenzori)	X:			
⎧ HUMU (ki-)	a	⎧ AMBA (ku-) (kw-amba)	AMBA	D.22/0 Hamba, Bulebule
⎨ HYANZI (ki-)	b	⎨ HYANZI̧ (ki-) SUWA (ku-)		
⎩ LEGA (clan)	c			

MBUTI (ku- or ki-), spoken by BAMBUTI Pygmies

Where spoken: C.B., scattered among the forest ba-BILA. Their speech has certain peculiarities which render it easily identifiable (especially as regards pronunciation) (NBii).

KAIKU (i-)

Where spoken: C.B., in the Beni area, on the Beni–Mambasa road.

BILA (forest) (ku̧-bi̧ṛa)

Where spoken: C.B., Terr. Beni and Epulu.
Number: 5,659 in Terr. Beni (NBii).

---

[1] Tucker, personal communication. [2] Ibid. [3] Lyndon Harries, personal communication.

BIRA GROUP

KUUMU (ki-)

Where spoken: C.B., over a wide area: Lubutu and R. Lowa; Terr. Bafwasende, between R. Tshopo and R. Maika; north of Stanleyville; on the Stanleyville–Benyamusa road (spoken by the ba-DOOMBI or ba-KUUMU, previously wrongly classified as non-Bantu-speaking BARUMBI); Terr. Opienge; Terr. Ponthierville.

Number: Lubutu 34,383, Stanleyville 11,752, Opienge 3,370, Ponthierville *c.* 10,000 (NBii).

Only the northern fringe of the area was investigated by the NBBS team.

BILI (i-)

Where spoken: C.B., Terr. Lubero, north of Biambi.
Number: 5,139 (NBii).

The following dialects were noted:
BILI;
LEEDJI of Manguredzipa;
TIKE of Mt. Mayi.

Other dialects are said to be spoken by:
ba-BAIDUMBA of Avakubi;
ba-BEKA of Fungula Meso;
ba-HOKOHOKO of Lubema.

BUGOMBE (e-)

Where spoken: C.B., Terr. Beni (*a*) between Lubena and the Beni–Bela road; (*b*) in an enclave on R. Semliki between Beni and Mutwanga.
Number: 12,304 (NBii).

This dialect closely resembles BILI.

The speech of the western ba-BIRA

Where spoken: C.B., Terr. Stanleyville and Ponthierville.
Number: Ponthierville 4,403 (NBii).

LENGOLA (ki-) and MITUKU (kinya-)

Where spoken: C.B. Terr. Ponthierville.

Classed by MG3 in a separate Group (see MBOLE-ENA Group, p. 103); according to Meeussen[1] they belong to the LEGA Group (see p. 92).

BIRA (ki-) (plains)

Where spoken: C.B., on Shari plain, 29° 50′–30° 20′ E., 1° 25′–1° 50′ N. (van Geluwe).[2]

'There is a marked difference between the speech of the forest Babila and that of the Babira of the plain' (NBii).

---

[1] 'De talen van Maniema (Belgisch Kongo)' (*Kongo-Overzee*, 1953).
[2] *Les Bira et les peuplades limitrophes* (Eth. Survey, 1957).

BIRA GROUP

BIRA (ki-) (Ruwenzori)

Where spoken: C.B., U., on the slopes of Ruwenzori.

NBii distinguishes three dialects:
 HUMU (AMBA);
 HYANZI;
 the speech of the LEGA clan.

NBiii groups together in one Cluster:
 HYANZI (ki-), on the C.B.–U. border on the slopes of Ruwenzori.
 AMBA (ku-), U., Toro D., north-west of Fort Portal on the western foothills of Ruwenzori.
  Number: 26,519 (1948 Census).
 SUWA (ku-), spoken by a few Pygmies among the AMBA.

LEGA GROUP

Where spoken: C.B., T.T.

	NBii		MG3		Other names
LEGA	Extr. E. Trans.		LƐGA (kẹ-)	D.25/*	Rega
†NYANGA		1	(NYANGA	D.43/o)	
			See NANDE Group, p. 95.		
KAANU (ki-)		2			
LEGA:		3			
⎧ LEEGA (ki-)		a			
⎪ LEEGA (i-)		b			
⎪ BEEMBE (e-)		c	(BEMBE (i-)	D.54/*)	BƐMBƐ (H54)
⎪			See SHI-HUNDE Group, p. 97.		
⎨ TUMBWE (e-)		d			
⎪ LEEGA (ki-)		e			
⎪ ⎧ SONGOLA (ke-)		f	SƆNGƆLA (kẹ-)	D.24/o	BINJA (Meeussen)[1]
⎪ ⎩ GENGELE (ke-)					
⎪ ⎧ ? SANZI (ki-)		g			
⎪ ⎨ BANGUBANGU (ki-)			BANGỌBANGỌ	D.27/o	
⎪			But see LUBA Group, p. 72.		
⎩ BUYU (ki-)					BUJWE (Coupez)[2]
			ZĮMBA	D.26/o	? S. BINJA (Meeussen)
			HƆRƆHƆRƆ (ki-)	D.28/*	HOLOHOLO (ki-) (Coupez), Guha KALANGA (Coupez)
			(ƐNA	D.14/o)	GENYA (Meeussen), Enya
			See MBOLE-ENA Group, p. 103.		
			(LƐNGƆLA	D.12/o)	LENGOLA (Meeussen)
			See MBOLE-ENA and BIRA Groups, pp. 103, 89.		
			(MĮTŲKŲ	D.13/o)	METOKO (kenya-) (Meeussen), Mituku
			See MBOLE-ENA and BIRA Groups.		
					ZYOBA (Meeussen): ⎧ VIRA ⎩ MASANZE

MG3 also includes in this Group BALĮ (D.21/o)—see BALI Group, p. 88. AMBA (D.22/o) and KỌMỌ (D.23/o)—see BIRA Group.

[1] 'De talen van Maniema (Belgisch Kongo).' [2] *Esquisse de la langue Holoholo* (1955).

LEGA GROUP

LEGA (kę-)

Where spoken: C.B., between the mid-Lualaba and the lakes, in an area bounded in the north by R. Lowa, in the south by R. Elila.

No accurate and definitive classification of the languages and/or dialects constituting this Group is possible, owing to the multiplicity of names used by different writers and the divergencies in extant classifications. The NBBS team only investigated the dialects spoken near the northern Bantu borderline, and the list in NBii is therefore only partial.

NYANGA. But see NANDE Group, p. 95.

KAANU (ki-)

Where spoken: C.B., Terr. Masisi, in the Walikale area.

Number: 3,510.[1]

The 'Central LEGA bloc':

ki-LEEGA, spoken by the Shabunda BAKISI.

Number: 33,444.

i-LEEGA IMUZIMU, spoken in Terr. Mwenga.

BEEMBE, spoken in Terr. Uvira, on the shores of L. Tanganyika. But see SHI-HUNDE Group, p. 97.

TUMBWE, in Terr. Mwenga.

Number: 7,997.

According to NBii this dialect appears to differ but little from BEEMBE; Coupez, however, groups it with HOLOHOLO (see below).

ki-LEEGA kya Wakabango of Fundi Sadi.

Not investigated by the NBBS team.

SONGOLA of R. Lowa.

According to Meeussen a part of the SONGOLA people[2] speak BINJA, which belongs to the LEGA Group and is especially closely related to BEMBE (see above) and BUYU (see below).

GENGELE (ke-)

and perhaps also:

SANZI (ki-) of Baraka, including

BANGUBANGU (but see LUBA Group, p. 72).

BUYU (ki-), described by Meeussen as closely related to BINJA and BEMBE; by Coupez as closely related to HOLOHOLO.

ZĮMBA

Where spoken: C.B. slightly inland from the right bank of the middle Lualaba between R. Elila and 4° 20' S., eastwards to 28° 40' E., in a narrow belt north of 4° S.

Number: 50,000 (VBRL).

This is perhaps the Southern BINJA of Meeussen.

[1] Figures for this Group from NBii (C.B.), 1948 Census (T.T.), unless otherwise stated.
[2] The other part of the SONGOLA speak ɔMBɔ (see TETELA Group, p. 52).

LEGA GROUP

HOLOHOLO (ki-)

Where spoken: T.T., C.B. (and U.), on the eastern and western shores of L. Tanganyika, and north and south of Albertville in 'ancien Katanga'.

Number: T.T. 2,109.

KALANGA

Considered as closely related to HOLOHOLO by Coupez.

To the 'LEGA complex' Meeussen adds:

GENYA—see MBOLE-ENA Group, p. 103.

LENGOLA and MITUKU—see MBOLE-ENA and BIRA Groups, pp. 103, 89.
also perhaps:

ZYOBA, consisting of:

VIRA and MASANZE
Where spoken: On L. Tanganyika.

NANDE GROUP

Where spoken: C.B., U.

The name NANDE (of unknown origin) is in common use as a general term covering a number of dialects, including those also known as YIRA (NBii).

NBii			NBiii	MG3	Other names
YIRA (eki-) Extr. E., C.:					
BITO (eki-)	I	a			
HIRA (eki-)		b			
HOMBA (eki-)		c			
N. NANDE	II			NDANDI (oru-) D.42/*	Nandi, Ndande
NANDE	III:				
MATE (eki-)		a			
KUMBULE (eki-)		b			
TANGI (eki-)		c			
SWAGA	IV:				
SWAGA (eki-)		a			
KIRA (eki-)		b			
SHU	V:				
SHU (eki-)		a			
?SHUKAALI (eki-)		b			
LEGA (eki-)	VI	a			
HAMBO (eki-)		b			
SONGOORA (eki-)	VII				
SANZA (eki-)	VIII				
			KƆNZƆ (olu-)	KONZO (olu-) D.41/*	Konjo, Kondjo
			KOBI (ru-)		Hunde
†(NYANGA)				NYANGA D.43/0	
See also LEGA Group, p. 92.					

YIRA (or NANDE) dialects

'The natives insist that there are many localized dialects, but the differences between them are very slight' (NBii).

Three dialects are listed in NBii under YIRA (see list above).

Dialects spoken by the northern ava-NANDE in Terr. Beni.
Number: 1,735.[1]

NANDE dialects:

MATE (eki-), in Terr. Lubero.
Number: 19,151.

[1] Figures for this Group from NBii, unless otherwise stated.

NANDE GROUP

KUMBULE (eki-), in Terr. Masisi.
Number: 3,293.
TANGI (eki-), in Terr. Lubero.

SWAGA dialects:

SWAGA (eki-), in Terr. Lubero.
Number: 121,246.
KIRA (eki-)

SHU dialects:

SHU (eki-), in Terr. Beni, over a wide area.
Number: 64,689.
? SHUKAALI (eki-), spoken by the ba-SHU women, who are known as ava-SHUKAALI.

LEGA (eki-) (no location given).[1]

HAMBO (eki-) (no location given).

SONGOORA (eki-)

Where spoken: On the shores of L. Edward at the mouth of R. Semliki.
Number: Terr. Beni 1,266.
The SONGOORA claim that they formerly spoke a NYORO dialect (NBii).

SANZA (eki-)

Where spoken: C.B. and U., scattered around Beni in several small groups.
Number: *c*. 15,000.
According to NBii these people are called ba-KONDJO ('people with filed teeth'), especially in Uganda. But see below.

NBiii groups the following two units with YIRA:

KƆNZƆ (olu-)

Where spoken: U., high on the slopes of Ruwenzori.
Number: 73,745 (1948 Census).
Also said to be spoken by the people called aba-NYAISUUBI by the Tooro, on the hills west of L. Edward, near Mpondwe customs post.

KOBỊ (ru-)

Where spoken: U., in a small enclave in Kigezi D.

†NYANGA

Where spoken: C.B. Terr. Masisi, north of Masisi.
Number: 24,744.
Classed as a LEGA dialect by Meeussen, but described by him as being loosely connected with LEGA, but perhaps more with NANDE.[2]

[1] To be distinguished from LEGA Group (p. 92).
[2] 'De talen van Maniema (Belgisch Kongo).'

SHI-HUNDE GROUP

Where spoken: C.B.

	NBii		MG3		Other names
SHI	Extr. E., D.:				
⎧HAAVU (eki-)	I	a	HAVU	D.52/0	
⎪⎧SHI		b 1–3			
⎪⎪LINDJA		4			
⎨⎨ZIBA		5			
⎪⎪HWINDJA		6			Lwindja
⎩⎩LONGE-LONGE		7			
HUNDE	II:				
TEMBO:		a	NYABUNGU	D.53/0	
⎧TEMBO (ki-)		1			
⎩HUNDE (ki-)		2	HUNDE	D.51/*	
NYINDU:		b			
⎧NYINDU (ki-)		1			
⎩? RHINYIRHINYI (eki-)		2			
			BEMBE (i-)	D.54/*	
			But see LEGA Group, p. 92.		
			BUYI	D.55/0	
			KABWARI	D.56/0	
FULIRO (VBRL)			(FULIRO	D.63/*)	FULIIRU (iki-) (Meeussen),[1] Furiiro
			See HA Group, p. 100.		

According to Meeussen this Group is closely related to the Inter-Lacustrine Group (see p. 104).

HAAVU (eki-)

Where spoken: Terr. Kalehe, chefferies Kashofu, Binga, and Kaliba, and especially on Kidzwi Island.
Number: 50,000.

SHI

Where spoken: Terr. Kabare and Mwenga.
NBii distinguishes the following dialects:
  The speech of Kabare.
    Number: 80,000.
    'Reputedly the purest and most common form' of SHI (NBii).
  The speech of Burhale–Ngweshi.
    Number: 109,784.

[1] Personal communication.

Very close to the 'Kabare' form.
The speech of Nyangeshi south of Bukavu (influenced by the admixture of thousands of immigrant workers).

LINDJA, in Terr. Kabare.
Number: 4,601.

ZIBA, in Terr. Kabare.
Number: 8,982.

HWINDJA, in Terr. Mwenga.
Number: 8,193.

LONGE-LONGE, in the north of Terr. Kabare.

TEMBO (ki-)

Where spoken: West of L. Kivu, north and south of the SHI area.
NBii distinguishes two dialects:
TEMBO, especially in the Kalehe area (a few speakers may be found mingled with other tribes as far as Terr. Masisi).
Number: 15,020.
HUNDE (ki-), in the east of Terr. Rutshuru and in a large part of Terr. Masisi.
Number: 33,583.

NYINDU (ki-)

Where spoken: Terr. Mwenga.
According to NBii there are 'two languages, which diverge only slightly and seem to contain certain archaic survivals':

NYINDU (ki-)
Number: 11,000.
? RHINYIRHINYI (eki-) of Burhinyi
Number: 14,393.

MG3 adds to this Group:

BEMBE. But see LEGA Group, p. 92.

BUYI

Where spoken: Along the upper Luama river and on the shore of L. Tanganyika at 5° S.

KABWARI

Where spoken: On the north-western shore of L. Tanganyika, between 4° and 5° S.
Note that VBRL refers to ki-BWARI, also ki-YOBA (YOA), ki-SANZI and ki-GOMA, of which the available linguistic material (vocabularies only) is insufficient for classification. He adds that many speakers of these small languages or dialects may have lost their own speech in favour of SHI or LEGA.

VBRL also adds to this Group:

FULIRO

Where spoken: In an area about 30 miles wide at the northern end of L. Tanganyika west of R. Ruzizi.
Number: *c.* 56,100 (VBRL, from 1932 Census).
Classed by MG3 in the HA Group (p. 100).

HA GROUP[1]

Where spoken: T.T.

	MG3	Other names
SHUBI (uru-)	D.64/*	Subi, Sinja
HANGAZA	D.65/*	
HA (iki-)	D.66/*	
VINZA	D.67/o	
FULIRO	D.63/*	

See also SHI-HUNDE Group, p. 97.

MG3 also includes RUANDA (D.61) and RUNDI (D.62). See Inter-Lacustrine Group, p. 104.

SHUBI (uru-)

Where spoken: On the Ruanda-Urundi border about 2° 30′ S.
Number: 74,052.[2]

HANGAZA

Where spoken: About 2° 20′ S., 31° E.
Number: 54,425.

HA (iki-)

Where spoken: On the eastern shores of L. Tanganyika, from the northern end of the lake to within 20 miles of Ujiji, eastwards to the swamps at the headwaters of R. Mikonga.
Number: 286,112.
Formerly used in education and religious teaching by German missions.

VINZA

Where spoken: In a belt about 30 miles wide along 5° S., between 30° and 31° E.
Number: 3,075.

FULIRO. But see also SHI-HUNDE Group, p. 97.

---

[1] Called RUANDA-RUNDI Group in MG3. As, however, these two units are here placed in another Group, the name of the language spoken by the greatest number of people has been chosen as the Group name.

[2] Figures for this Group from 1948 Census.

NYALI GROUP

Where spoken: C.B., U.

	NBii		NBiii	MG3		*Other names*
NYALI (li-) E. Trans.	I:					Nyari
⎡BVANUMA (li-)		a	VANUMA			S. Nyali,
⎟			(lį-vanuma)			Bambutuku
⎨NYALI (li-)		b	NYALI			N. Nyali
⎟			(lį-nyalı)			
⎣BOMBI (li-)		c				
				HUKU (li-)	D.33/0	Hoko
BUDU (e-)	II:					
⎡MATTA	a					
⎟ ⎰BAFWAKAYI	b					
⎟ ⎱MALAMBA						
⎨BAFWAGADA	c					Lega
⎟ MAKODA, &c.	d					
⎣BALIKA	e					
MBO (i-, ki-)	III					
NDAAKA (i-)	IV					
BEEKE (i-)	V					

NYALI (li-)
 Where spoken: C.B., U., in two areas (see below), separated by the LENDU (non-Bantu-speaking).
 Dialects:
VANUMA (li-)
 Where spoken: C.B., Terr. Geti, Dzabi chefferie, southwards as far as Mboga and westwards to the Irumu–Beni road; U., in AMBA territory on the slopes of Ruwenzori.
 Number: 1,927.[1]

NYALI (li-)
 Where spoken: C.B., Terr. Djugu, in an enclave among non-Bantu speakers.
 Number: 10,679.

BOMBI (li-), spoken by a group of northern ba-NYALI in C.B., Terr. Watsa, in the Arebi area, appears to be NYALI under another name.

HUKU is either another name for NYALI, or that of a closely related dialect.[2]

BUDU (e-)
 Where spoken: C.B., Terr. Wamba.
 Number: 83,329.

---

[1] Figures for this Group from NBii.
[2] VBRL. Note that the name HUKU is also associated with a branch of the MVU'BA (MBUBA) (non-Bantu-speaking).

NBii distinguishes dialects spoken by:
  MATTA, north and south of Maboma;
  BAFWAKAYI and MALAMBA, north of Bafwabaka;
  BAFWAGADA, between Bafwabale and Ibambe;
  MAKODA, WADIMBISA and TIMONIKO, in the Ibambe area;
  BALIKA, in Malika–Mabudu chefferie.

MBO (i- or ki-)

Where spoken: C.B., Terr. Epulu.
Number: 2,060.

NDAAKA (i-)

Where spoken: C.B., Terr. Epulu, in the Avakubi area, but extending north to R. Ituri.
Number: 4,750.

BEEKE (i-)

Where spoken: C.B., in two villages (*a*) on the Avakubi–Irumu road; (*b*) south of R. Ituri.

MBOLE-ENA GROUP?

Where spoken: C.B.

MG3

MBƆLƐ	D.11/0	But see MONGO-NKUNDO Group, p. 48.
LƐNGƆLA	D.12/0	But see BIRA and LEGA Groups, pp. 89, 92.
MĮTŲKŲ	D.13/0	But see BIRA and LEGA Groups.
ƐNA	D.14/0	But see LEGA Group.

The existence of this Group is very uncertain, all the units in it being placed in other Groups by various authorities.

Of ENYA (ƐNA), NBii says: 'The investigation of the language spoken by the Ba-enya now shows clearly that its speakers are of foreign origin. It belongs to the central Bantu language bloc.' The ba-ENYA or wa-GENIA are fisherfolk of Stanleyville.

INTER-LACUSTRINE GROUP[1]

Where spoken: T.T., R.-U., C.B., U., K.

NBii	NBiii and Tucker[2]	MG3		Other names
		JITA (eci-)	E.25/*	Kwaya
	{KEREBE (eci-)	KEREBE (eki-)	E.24/*	Kerebe, Kerewe
	{KARA			
		DZINDZA (eci-)	E.23/*	Jinja, Zinza, Zinja, Ziba
	HAYA (olu-)	HAYA (eki-)	E.22:	
	ZIBA (olu-)	{ZIBA (eki-)[3]	E.22/*	
		{HAMBA	E.22/o	
		{HANGIRO	E.22/o	
		{NYAKISASA	E22/o	
		{YOZA	E.22/o	
		{EDANGABO	E.22/o	
		{BUMBIRA	E.22/o	
		{MWANI	E.22/o	
	KOOKI (olu-)			
RUNDI	RUNDI (iki-)	(RUNDI (iki-)	D.62/*)	
Extr. E., B. II				
RWANDA: B. I	(NYA) RWANDA (uru-nya-rwanda)	(RUANDA (uru-nya-)	D.61/*)	Nyaruanda, Runyarwanda
{RWANDA a				
{(iki-nya-)				
{{NDUGA 1				
{{(iki-nya-)				
{{NDARA (i-) 2				
{{GANZA (i-) 3				S. Buganza
{{NDORWA 4				Rukiga, Ruciga
{{(i-)				
{KIGA (igi-) b	(see KIGA below)			
{Bufumbwa c				
{HUTU d				
{{NDARA 1				
{{LERA (uru-) 2				Hera (iki-)
{{SHOBYO 3				
{{(iki-)				
{{{TSHOGO 4				Ndogo (ki-)
{{{(i-)				
{{{TSHIGA				Kiga (uru-, i-)
{{{(igi-)				
	TWA (ru-tkwa)			

[1] MG3's NYORO-GANDA and HAYA-JITA Groups combined.
[2] Personal communication.   [3] List of HAYA dialects from MG1.

INTER-LACUSTRINE GROUP

NBii		NBiii and Tucker	MG3	Other names
HIMA (oru-):				Huma, Hema
Extr. E., A. IV				
⎧ HEMA (oru-)	a			
⎪ HUMA (oru-)	b			
⎨ HEMA (ki-)	c			
⎩ HIMA (oru-)	d			
⎧ NYAMBO	V		NYAMBO (eki-) E.21/*	Karagwe
⎨ (ru-)				
⎪ KARAGWE				Ururagwe
⎩ (ru-)				
⎧ BWISI	III	⎧ BWISI (oɾu-ʊwɪsɪ)		Mawisi
⎨		⎨		
⎩ TALINGE (ki-)		⎩ TALINGA (ki-)		
		KIGA (oru-tʃiga)	CIGA (olu-) E.14/*	Chiga
		(NYA) NKORE (oru-nya-ŋkore):	NYANKOLE (olu-) E.13/*	Lunyankole, Nkole
		⎧ HIMA		Huma
		⎪ IRU		Yiru
HORORO (etshi-)	VI	⎨ HORORO (ru-)		Horohoro
		⎪ TAGWENDA (oru-)		Takwenda
		⎧ TOORO (oru-)	TORO (oru-) E.12/*	
		⎩ NYORO (oru-)	NYORO (oru-) E.11/*	Gungu, Kyopi
		GANDA (olu-)	GANDA (olu-) E.15/*	Luganda
		SOGA (olu-)	SOGA (olu-) E.16/*	
		SESE (olu-)		
		GWERE (lu-)	GWERE (olu-) E.17/*	
		KENYI (lu-)		
		SYAN (oru-)		'Bantu Sabei'
		NYALA (olu-)	NYALA (olu-) E.18/*	Nyara
		But see also LUHYA Group, p. 111.		
		? SINGA (lu-)		

The units in this Group are here dealt with in roughly geographical order round L. Victoria, south-east–west–north–north-east.

Population figures from 1948 Census, unless otherwise stated.

JITA (eci-) (KWAYA)

Where spoken: T.T., on the south-eastern shore of L. Victoria between R. Mara in the north and 2° 10′ in the south, and inland for 60–70 miles.

Number: JITA 71,433, KWAYA 25,657.

KEREBE. Two dialects may be distinguished:
   KEREBE (eci-)
   Where spoken: T.T., on Bukerebe Island, on adjacent islands, and on the Bukerebe peninsula.
   Number: 31,260.

KARA
   Where spoken: T.T., on the mainland opposite Bukerebe Island.
   Number: 30,685.

DZINDZA (eci-)
   Where spoken: T.T., on the south-western shore of L. Victoria from the corner of the lake for about 100 miles eastwards, 70 miles north, 60 miles west to the Ruanda border.
   Number: 60,653 (the Uganda Census also gives 5,882 ZINJA).

HAYA (eki-)
   Where spoken: T.T., U., on the western shore of L. Victoria from the mouth of R. Kagera to 2° S., and westwards to the Ruanda border.
   Number: 264,142.
   MG1 distinguishes a number of dialects (see list above), including ZIBA. This name, however, also occurs as an alternative name for HAYA.

KOOKI (olu-)
   Where spoken: U., in a small enclave east of Mbarara.
   Number: Very few.
   The language is dying out; local informants state that it resembles HAYA (Tucker).

RUNDI (iki-)
   Where spoken: R.-U., in the northern part of Urundi to just south of the northern end of L. Tanganyika, extending into U., T.T., and C.B. (Terr. Uvira).
   Number: Urundi 2,024,925 (NBii), T.T. 90,312, U. 56,504, C.B. 12,943 (NBii.) NBii also notes: 'Of the combined labour force of 14,371 Banyarwanda and Barundi now employed in the Belgian Congo we are unable to say what proportion are Barundi.'
   RUNDI is used in general and religious education.
   The ba-RUNDI consist of two social classes, the ba-TUTSI (wa-TUSSI, TUSI) and the ba-HUTU. The ba-TUTSI speak with an 'aristocratic', the ba-HUTU with a 'common', accent. The 'standard' form of the language is that of the HUTU (Tucker). See also under RWANDA.

RWANDA (iki-nya- or oru-nya-)
   Where spoken: R.-U., in Ruanda; also in U., Kigezi D., in T.T., and in C.B., Terr. Rutshuru and Masisi.
   Number: Ruanda 1,870,410 (NBii), C.B. 105,824—a proportion of the immigrant labour force (NBii), U. 289,051 (including immigrant labour), T.T. 18,214.
   Used in general and religious education.
   As in the case of the RUNDI, the people calling themselves banya-RWANDA consist of two social classes, the ba-TUTSI and ba-HUTU, both owing allegiance to

the one Mwami (King). The ba-TUTSI speak with an 'aristocratic', the ba-HUTU with a 'common', accent. The difference is sufficient to affect spelling. The form chosen for the Bible is that used by the HUTU (Tucker).

NBii distinguishes the following dialects in C.B. and adjacent areas:

RWANDA 'proper':
NDUGA (iki-nya-), at Nyanza;
NDARA (i-), at Kisangala;
GANZA (i-), at Rwamagana;
NDORWA (i-), at Biumba.

KIGA (igi-) of Bwisha.

The speech of Bufumbwa in Uganda.

The speech of the ba-HUTU (but see above), including:
NDARA, at Kisagala;
LERA (uru-), at Rwasa;
SHOBYO (iki-) at Nyundo;
TSHOGO (i-) and TSHIGA (igi-), spoken by the ba-TSHIGA in the mountains of Murunda.

TWA (ru-), spoken by the 'BATWA' Pygmies living among the RWANDA in U., Kisoro D., is a debased form of RWANDA (Tucker).

RUNDI and RWANDA are usually classed as separate languages, because they are acknowledged as such by their speakers, but they are extremely closely interrelated. NBii states that 'the unification of Ikinyarwanda and Ikirundi is eminently desirable and, moreover, capable of being achieved very rapidly if local collisions are avoided. It is a psychological rather than a linguistic problem.'

HIMA

According to NBii 'the Avahima shepherds who emigrated from Unyoro to the west of L. Albert have almost all lost their original language'.

The following dialects were, however, noted in C.B. and Ruanda:

HEMA (oru-), in Terr. Bunia in a few villages in the Bagota chefferie of Sota.
Number: 2,295 (NBii).

HUMA (oru-), in Terr. Bunia around Badia (spoken by the aba-BITO clan).

HEMA (ki-), in one village in the extreme south of Terr. Djugu.
Number: 1,450.

HIMA (oru-), in the extreme north of Ruanda.

See also HIMA under NKORE, p. 108.

NYAMBO (ru-)

Where spoken: T.T., in a small area about 30 miles each way, south of R. Kagera, and in a few hamlets in Ruanda.

Number: T.T. 3,950, including KARAGWE.

KARAGWE (ru-)

Where spoken: In the same area as NYAMBO.

These two speeches are not distinguished as separate in MG3.

BWISI-TALINGA Dialect Cluster: BWISI (oru-) and TALINGA (ki-)

Where spoken: U., in AMBA territory on the north-western foothills of Ruwenzori; C.B., Terr. Beni.

Number: C.B. 5,945 (NBii).

KIGA (oru-)

Where spoken: U., around Kabale and L. Bunyoni, on the Ruanda border.

Number: 271,738.

Used in sub-standard education.

NKORE (oru-nya-)

Where spoken: U., between L. Edward and L. George in the west, R. Kagera in the south, and 31° 20′ E. in the east.

Number: 387,529.

Used in primary education.

The ba-HIMA social class speak NKORE with an 'aristocratic' accent, i.e. with distinctions of pronunciation which are reflected in spelling. The speech of the ba-IRU, the lower social class, has more in common with KIGA, and also with TOORO, than has the HIMA form. Both groups of people, however, owe allegiance to the one Omugabe (King) (Tucker).

A variant form of NKORE spoken in Mpororo and known as HORORO, has been regarded by some authorities as a separate language[1] (Tucker). This is the HORORO of NBii, also spoken in a few villages in C.B., north of Biumba.

There is also a variant of NKORE known as TAGWENDA, spoken in the north of the NKORE area bordering on Butoro. It is influenced by TOORO (Tucker).

NYORO-TOORO Dialect Cluster:

TOORO (oru-)

Where spoken: U., at the southern end of L. Albert on the eastern flanks of Ruwenzori, eastwards almost to Mubende.

Number: 162,659.

TOORO is also spoken by the KONZO who have come down to the plains from Ruwenzori, and by many BWISI.

NYORO (oru-)

Where spoken: U., mainly in Bunyoro D., between L. Albert and L. Kyoga south of the Victoria Nile, but extending southwards beyond R. Kafu in the no-man's-land near Mubende.

Number: 180,610.

Used in sub-standard education.

GANDA (olu-)

Where spoken: U., Buganda D., north and north-west of L. Victoria, in an area bounded in the south-west by the lower Kagera river, in the east by the Victoria Nile,

[1] Perhaps through confusion with HOLOHOLO (see LEGA Group, p. 92).

in the west by 21° 20′ E. There are also colonies of GANDA around most of the government posts: Mbale, Arua, Seroti, Kaberamaido, &c.

Number: 836,091; there are about 5,500 GANDA in T.T.

Used as a medium of general intercourse over a considerable area, and in education in vernacular schools and to some extent in secondary schools.

There is a considerable vernacular literature, including some newspapers.

SOGA (olu-)

Where spoken: U., Busoga D., east of the Victoria Nile, south of L. Kyoga.
Number: 426,608.

Two dialectal variants have been distinguished, spoken in the northern and southern parts of the area respectively.

SESE (olu-)

Where spoken: U., on the Sese archipelago in L. Victoria.

The SESE dialects differ from island to island. There are also dialects on other islands, e.g. olu-VUMA on Buvuma Island and olu-GAYA on Bugaya Island.

These dialects seem to have more in common with NYORO than with either GANDA or SOGA.

GWERE (lu-)

Where spoken: U., in a small area at the eastern end of L. Kyoga.
Number: 83,223.

KENYI (lu-)

Where spoken: U., near the GWERE area.

SYAN (oru-)

Where spoken: U., north of Mbale in the Legenyi area of north-eastern Bugishu (Huntingford).[1]

Number: Estimated at *c.* 10,000 by Huntingford in 1925. Whether the SYAN still exist as a separate entity is not known for certain.

SYAN contains many NANDI (non-Bantu) words.

NYALA (olu-)

Where spoken: K., in a small area on the north-eastern shore of L. Victoria west of Mjanji.

This language might, however, be related to the speech of the NYALA (see LUHYA Group, p. 111).

SINGA (lu-), spoken on Rusinga Island in the Kavirondo Gulf, would appear, from Johnston's material, to belong to this Group. Whiteley, however,[1] states that the people on this and neighbouring islands now speak LUO (non-Bantu), but that there seems to be a small group of people still speaking an archaic form of GANDA.

[1] Personal communication.

GISU GROUP (OR SINGLE UNIT?)

Where spoken: U., K.

NBiii	MG3		*Other names*
GISU, GISHU (ulu-):	GISU (lu-)	E.31a/*	Masaba
⎧ Northern			
⎪ DADIRI (ulu-)			
⎨ BUYA (ulu-)			
⎩ ? KISU (ulu-)	KISU (ulu-)	E.31b/*	
BUKUSU (ulu-)	BUKUSU (ulu-)	E.31c/*	Kitosh

GISU (ulu-)

Where spoken: U., K., west of Mt. Elgon.
Number: U. 243,742, K. 9,681 (possibly including BUKUSU).[1]
At least three dialects are known to exist:
   The northern dialect;
   DADIRI (central);
   BUYA (southern);
   and perhaps also KISU, south of Mt. Elgon.
The name MASABA is sometimes applied to some of the GISU-speaking people and their language; MG3 uses it as the name of the whole Cluster.

BUKUSU (ulu-)

Where spoken: K., south of Mt. Elgon in the northern corner of the 'Bantu Kavirondo pocket'.[2]

It is not certain whether KISU and BUKUSU are to be considered as separate units, or as dialects of the GISU Cluster (NBiii).

[1] Figures for this Group from 1948 Census.
[2] The name 'Bantu Kavirondo pocket' refers to an enclave of Bantu-speaking peoples (mainly speakers of LUHYA languages or dialects) between the LUO on the south and the JOPADHOLA and speakers of NANDI dialects on the north.

LUHYA GROUP

Where spoken: U., K.

NBiii	MG3		Other names
NYULI (olu-)	NYULI (olu-)	E.35/*	
LUHYA, LUYIA:			Luluhya, Luluyia
⎧ SAAMIA (lu-)	SAAMIA (olu-)	E.34/*	Samia, Samya
⎪ ? GWE (lu-)			
⎪ XAAYO (lu-)			Khayo, Tindi
⎪ MARACI (lu-)			
⎪ HANGA (lu-)	HANGA (olu-)	E.32:	Kawanga
⎪	WANGA (olu-)	E.32a/*	
⎪ TSOOTSO (lu-)	TSOTSO	E.32b/o	
⎨ KAKELELWA (lu-)			Lewi
⎪ NYALA (lu-)			
⎪ But see also Inter-Lacustrine Group, p. 104.			
⎪ ISUXA (lw-)			Isukha ⎫ Kakamega,
⎪ IDAXO (lw-)			Idakho, ⎬ Kakumega
⎪			Itokho ⎭
⎪ TIRIKI (lu-)			
⎪ MARAMA (lu-)			
⎪ KISA (lu-ʃisa)			
⎪ NYOLE (lu-nyoɾe)	NYORE (olu-)	E.33/*	Nyoole
⎩ TACONI			Tatsoni, Tadjoni

NYULI (olu-)

Where spoken: U., in a small area south of Mbale, in Busoga and Mbale Districts (the only unit in this Group not spoken in the 'Bantu Kavirondo pocket').

Number: 56,975.[1]

LUHYA, LUYIA (lu-)

Speakers of these dialects have adopted the name LUHYA or LUYIA[2] (both versions being in current use) as a general name covering several tribes and their dialects.

Number: K. 653,774 (this figure probably includes speakers of all those dialects for which no separate figures are given). There are a few thousand LUHYA in U.

The following dialects have been distinguished:[3]

SAAMIA (lu-)

Where spoken: U., K., on the northern shore of L. Victoria, extending northwards for about 25 miles.

Number: U. c. 16,000, K. 43,377.

---

[1] Figures for this Group from 1948 Census.

[2] The name means 'fellow clansmen' and is said to have originated among the HANGA. It has been in general use since about 1940.

[3] NBiii, largely from information supplied by G. W. B. Huntingford and A. Maleche. Vernacular names from Maleche (a mw-IDAXO).

LUHYA GROUP

GWE (lu-)

Where spoken: U., in the central part of SAAMIA country.

It is not certain whether GWE should be considered as a separate dialect, or a variant of SAAMIA.

XAAYO (lu-)
MARACI (lu-) } in the central and western part of the 'Bantu Kavirondo pocket'.
HANGA (lu-)

TSOOTSO (lu-)
KAKELELWA (lu-) } in the eastern part of the 'Bantu Kavirondo pocket'.
NYALA (lu-)

ISUXA (lw-)
IDAXO (lw-) } in the south-eastern part of the 'Bantu Kavirondo pocket'.

TIRIKI (lu-), between the IDAXO and the NANDI-speaking TERIK.

MARAMA (lu-)
KISA (lu-) } between the NYOOLE and the HANGA.

TACONI, east of the BUKUSU area.

GUSII GROUP[1]

Where spoken: K., T.T.

NBiii	MG3		*Other names*
LUGOOLJ (l-)	LLOGOLE	E.41/*	Ragoli, Maragoli
GUSJI[2]	GUSJI (eke-)	E.42/*	Gusii, Guzii, Kisii, Kosova
KURJA (eki-)	KORJA (eke-)	E.43/*	Kuria, Kurya, Tende
	⎧ SWETA	E.44/o[3]	
	⎨ KIROBA	E.44/o	
	⎩ SJMBJTJ	E.44/o	
NGURIMI (ɪkɪ-ŋgʊrɪmɪ)			Ngoreme, Ngruimi, Nguruimi
ZANAKI	ZANAKI:	E.44/o	
	⎧ ZANAKJ (iki-)		
	⎪ ? JSENYJ (iki-)		
	⎨ NDALI		
	⎪ SJORA		
	⎪ ? JKJZU		
	⎩ ? GIRANGO		
NATA (ɪkɪ-)	NATA (iki-)	E.45/*	Ikoma
? WARE			

MG3 also includes SONJO (E.46). But see KIKUYU Group, p. 115.

LOGOOLJ (l-)

Where spoken: K., north of the Kavirondo Gulf in the southern part of the 'Bantu Kavirondo pocket'.
Used in sub-standard education.

GUSJI

Where spoken: K., in the highlands south of the Kavirondo Gulf to about 10° S., including Kisii in the west.
Number: 255,108; also 3,361 in T.T.[4]

KURJA (eki-)

Where spoken: T.T., in the extreme north of Musoma D.; K., in the southern part of S. Nyanza D. (where it is known as TENDE).
Number: T.T. 65,388, K. 28,873.

---

[1] Called RAGOLI-KURIA Group in MG3. The name used here is that of the language spoken by the largest number of people.
[2] The pronunciation of the name varies greatly, e.g. ekɪ-gʊsjj (ɪkɪ-), ekɪ-gusjj, &c. (Whiteley, personal communication).   [3] Lists of KORJA and ZANAKI dialects from MG1.
[4] Figures for this Group from 1948 Census.   [5] Personal communication.

According to Whiteley[5] the following (listed in MG1 under ZANAKI) are dialects of KURIA:

SWETA;
KIROBA;
SIMBITI.

NGURIMI (ɪkɪ-)

Where spoken: T.T., on the south bank of R. Mara.
Number: 11,800.

ZANAKI (iki-)

Where spoken: T.T., in S. Mara D., west of the NGURIMI, south of the KURIA.
Number: 22,736.

MG1 lists the following dialects (together with some which are here classed as KURIA—see above):

ZANAKI
ISENYI—queried by Whiteley;[1]
NDALI;
SIORA;
IKIZU—queried by Whiteley;
GIRANGO. According to Whiteley the GIRANGO ('those who have left the leopard clan') speak LUO.

NATA (iki-)

Where spoken: T.T., round Ikoma south of R. Mara, and westwards to 34° 10′ E.
Number: 9,487.

Nothing further is known of the WARE, who in Johnston's time were living on one of the islands in the Kavirondo Gulf, and whose speech may belong to this Group.

[1] Personal communication.

KIKUYU GROUP

Where spoken: K., T.T.

NBiii	MG3		Other names
GĨKUYU (γɪ-γɪkuyu)	GĘKOYO	E.51/*	Kikuyu
EMBU (ki-)	ƐMBO (kę-)	E.52/*	
MERU (ki-)	MƐRO (kę-)	E.53/*	
†THARAKA (kɪ-)¹	THARAKA	E.54/*	
†CHUKA			
See also TAITA Group, p. 125.			
KAMBA (kɪ-)	KAMBA (kę-)	E.55/	
DHAISO (ki-)	ḌAỊSO (kę-)	E.56/*	Sageju, Segeju, Sengeju
SONJO	(SONJO	E.46/o)	

GĨKUYU (gi-)

Where spoken: K., in the Kikuyu highlands between the upper Tana river and the slopes of Mt. Kenya, the south-western limit being the Nairobi area, the eastern 37° 50′ E.

Number: 1,026,341 including THARAKA, T.T. 1,772.²

Used in primary education, and as an alternative to SWAHILI in administration. There is considerable vernacular literature, including newspapers.

EMBU (ki-)

Where spoken: K., south-east of Mt. Kenya around Embu town.
Number: 203,690.

MERU (ki-)

Where spoken: K., north-west of Mt. Kenya, roughly as far north as Chandler's Falls on R. Uaso Nyiro, and eastwards to the Nyambeni hills.
Number: 324,894+25,040 in T.T.
Used in sub-standard education.
According to Lambert[3] MERU has affinities with the TAITA Group.

†THARAKA (ki-)

Where spoken: K., on the north bank of R. Tana just before it reaches the equator, 37° 50′–38° 30′ E.
Number: Included in KIKUYU in the 1948 Census; 16,505 (Lambert).[4]

According to Lambert THARAKA stands between the KIKUYU and TAITA Groups (see p. 125).

†According to Lambert[5] the speech of the CHUKA in Meru D. likewise stands between the KIKUYU and TAITA Groups.
Number: 18,480.

[1] TH is used here to represent the sound θ, and to distinguish it from t+h, as in SOTHO.
[2] Figures for this Group from 1948 Census, unless otherwise stated.
[3] Quoted in Middleton, *The Kikuyu and Kamba of Kenya* (Eth. Survey, 1953).
[4] Ibid.   [5] Ibid.

KIKUYU GROUP

KAMBA (ki-)

Where spoken: K., south of R. Tana from the equator to its source, thence eastwards to the Chyulu hills, and Mtito Andei.
Number: 611,725.
Used in primary education.

DHAISO (ki-)

Where spoken: T.T., on the coast north of Tanga; also (SEGEJU) in a small area at the foot of the Usambara hills.[1]
Considered by Lindblom[2] as a dialect of KAMBA.

SONJO[3]

Where spoken: T.T., in an enclave among the MAASAI, 1° 50′ S., 34° 40′ E., about 25 miles north-west of L. Natron.

---

[1] Dammann, 'Sprachproben aus dem Segedju' (*Z.E.S.*, 1937). He considers that the DHAISO on the coast no longer speak SEGEJU.
[2] Quoted in Middleton, op. cit.
[3] Information from Whiteley, personal communication.

SHAKA (CHAGGA) GROUP

Where spoken: T.T.

NBiii	MG3		Other names
KAHE (ki-)	KAHE (ki-)	E.64/*	
SHAKA (ki-):	CAGA	E.62:	Chaga, Chagga, Dschagga
⎧Vunjo, incl. Marangu	⎧WUNJO (ki-)	E.62b/*	Marangu
⎪MOCI (ki-motʃi)	⎪		Moshi
⎪MASHAMI (ki-)	⎪		Macame, Machame, Madschame
⎨SHIRA	⎨		
⎪ROMBO	⎪ROMBO (ki-)	E.62c/*	
⎪	⎩HAI (ki-)	E.62a/*	Meru[1]
⎩RWO (ki-)	RWO (ki-)	E.61/*	
GWENO	GWENO (ki-)	E.65/*	
RUSHA	RUSHA	E.63/0	Arusha,[2] Kuma

KAHE (ki-)

Where spoken: In the vicinity of Kahe junction south of Kilimanjaro.
Number: 1,801.[3]

SHAKA (ki-) (CHAGA)

Where spoken: On the eastern, southern, and western flanks of Kilimanjaro.
Number: 237,343 (excluding RWO).
The SHAKA dialects may conveniently be grouped as follows:[4]
  Dialects of Vunjo administrative division, of which that of Marangu may be taken as typical;
  MOCI, of old Moshi;
  SHIRA (own name not known);
  Dialects of Rombo administrative division;
  RWO, on the eastern slopes of Mt. Meru. The RWO are not administered with the SHAKA. Note that MG3 classes RWO as a separate language.
To these dialects MG3 adds HAI.

GWENO

Where spoken: On the northern slopes of the Pare mountains.
Number: Probably included in PARE (see ATHU, p. 122) in the Census.

RUSHA

Where spoken: In a small area south of Kahe.

[1] Not to be confused with MERU in the KIKUYU Group (see p. 115).
[2] The language of the 'Bantu-speaking ARUSHA'. Other people also known as ARUSHA, ARUSA, speak MAASAI.
[3] Figures for this Group from 1948 Census.
[4] NBiii, from information supplied by A. E. Sharp.

TONGWE GROUP?

Where spoken: T.T.

                MG3
           TONGWE (ki-)   F.11/*
           ? BENDE   F.12/o

TONGWE (ki-)

Where spoken: South of the lower Malagarasi river, west of R. Ugalla at their confluence, and westwards to within 30 miles of L. Tanganyika.

Number: 7,886.[1]

BENDE

Where spoken: In a small area about 30 miles from L. Tanganyika, extending to R. Ugalla and R. Uvinza.

Number: 6,827.

Nothing is known of this language.

[1] Figures for this Group from 1948 Census.

SUKUMA GROUP

Where spoken: T.T.

Bryan[1]	MG3		Other names
SUKUMA (ki-)	SUKUMA (ki-)	F.21/*	Gwe
KIYA			
NYAMWEZI (ki-)	NYAMWESI (ki-)	F.22:	Namwezi, Nyamwesi
⎧ NYANYƐMBƐ (ki-)	⎧ NYANYEMBE	F.22/*2	
⎪ TAKAMA	⎪ TAKAMA	F.22/o	Garaganza
⎨ MWERI (ki-na-)	⎨ MWERI	F.22/o	Sumbwa
⎩ KƆNƆNGƆ			
	⎩ KIYA (see above)	F.22/o	
	SUMBWA (ki-)	F.23/*	
⎰ KIMBU	KIMBU (ki-)	F.24/*	
⎱ BUNGU	BUNGU (iki-)	F.25/*	

SUKUMA (ki-)

Where spoken: South-east of L. Victoria, in an area bounded by Mwanza, Shinyanga, L. Eyasi, and 2° 20′ S., 55° E.

Number: 888,800.[3]

Used in primary education and religious instruction.

KIYA is the name given to an eastern dialect of SUKUMA, according to Chief Lugusha.

NYAMWEZI (ki-)

Where spoken: Over a large area with centre Tabora, from the north bank of R. Rungwa to 4° S., and at some points almost to L. Victoria.

Number: 362,829.

Dialects include:

NYANYƐMBƐ, in Tabora and surroundings;

TAKAMA, in the south-west;

MWERI or SUMBWA, on both banks of R. Nikonga, and northwards towards L. Victoria around Ushirombo.

Number: 58,143.

KƆNƆNGƆ, south-west of Tabora.

Number: 14,346.

SUKUMA and NYAMWEZI are very closely related, and might, linguistically, be considered as dialects of a Cluster; they are, however, regarded as separate languages by their speakers.

KIMBU (ki-)

Where spoken: South of the NYAMWEZI area, on the lower ground.

Number: 8,653.

BUNGU (iki-)

Where spoken: In much the same area as KIMBU, but on the higher plateau. These two dialects are almost identical.

[1] From information supplied by Chief Lugusha of Tabora.
[2] Dialects listed in MG1.
[3] Figures for this group from 1948 Census.

NILYAMBA GROUP[1]

Where spoken: T.T.

NBiii	MG3		Other names
NỊLYAMBA (kɪ-)	NỊLAMBA (ẹkẹ-)	F.31/*	Niramba, Iramba, Nilamba
RIMỊ (kɪ-ṛɪmị)	RẸMỊ (kẹ)	F.32/*	Limi, Rimi, Nyaturu
LANGỊ (kɪ-)	LANGỊ (kẹ-)	F.33/*	Irangi, Langi
? MBUGWE	MBUGWE	F.34/o	

NỊLYAMBA (kɪ-)

Where spoken: South of L. Eyasi, around Kinyangiri.
Number: 170,697.[2]
Used in mission schools.

RIMỊ (kɪ-)

Where spoken: In the southern part of the Singida area on both sides of the Manyoni–Kinyangiri railway, extending westwards to R. Wembere, eastwards to L. Balanigida Lelu.
Number: 181,739.

LANGỊ (kɪ-)

Where spoken: In an enclave among non-Bantu-speakers in Kondoa Irangi D.
Number: 95,422.

? MBUGWE

Where spoken: In an enclave among non-Bantu-speakers round L. Manyara, mainly to the east.
Number: 7,436.

---

[1] Called IRAMBA-IRANGI Group in MG3. [2] Figures for this Group from 1948 Census.

GOGO GROUP

Where spoken: T.T.

NBiii	MG3		Other names
GOGO (ci-)	GOGO (ci-)	G.11/*	
KAGULU (ci-)	KAGULU (ci-)	G.12/*	Kaguru, N. Sagara
MEGI (ci-)			

GOGO (ci-)

Where spoken: Dodoma D., north of R. Njombe and Great Ruaha river, 34°–36° 40′ E., extending north as far as 5° 20′ S.
Number: 271,254.[1]
Used in primary education in the early stages, and in religious instruction.

KAGULU (ci-)

Where spoken: North of Kilosa, 6° 30′ S., 37° E.
Number: 59,483.
Used in religious teaching and worship, mostly among the older people (SWAHILI being the language of education).
There are said to be two dialects, which differ slightly; the dialect called MEGI is that spoken at Berega mission.[2]

[1] Figures for this Group from 1948 Census.
[2] Information given to M.A.B. by local informants.

SHAMBAA GROUP

Where spoken: T.T., K.

NBiii	MG3		*Other names*
SHAMBAA (ki-)	SHAMBAA (ki-)	G.23/*	Shambala, Sambaa, Sambara, Schambala, &c.
BONDEI (ki-)	BONDEI (ki-)	G.24/*	Bonde
ATHU (ci-)	ATHU (ci-)	G.22/*	Asu, Chasu, Pare
TUBETA (ki-)	TUBETA (ki-)	G.21/*	Taveta

SHAMBAA (ki-)

Where spoken: T.T., in the Lushoto area north of R. Pangani as far as the Kenya border.
Number: 129,466.[1]

BONDEI (ki-)

Where spoken: T.T., in a small area behind the SWAHILI coastal fringe at Tanga, around Amani.
Number: 28,337.
BONDEI is very closely related to SHAMBALA, and considered as a dialect of it by DB.

ATHU (ci-)

Where spoken: T.T., on the Pare mountains, excluding the northern end.
Number: 98,959 PARE (this figure, however, probably includes the GWENO—see SHAKA Group, p. 117); 871 in K.

TUBETA (ki-)

Where spoken: K., south-east of Kilimanjaro, 3° 30′ S., 27° 50′ E.

DB classes ZIGULA (see ZARAMO Group, p. 123) in this Group. There is considerable resemblance between ZIGULA and SHAMBALA and BONDEI.[2]

[1] Figures for this Group from 1948 Census.   [2] Bryan, own researches.

ZARAMO GROUP

Where spoken: T.T.

MG3		DB	*Other names*
ZIGULA (ki-)	G.31/*	(ZIGULA)	Zigua, Zeguha
DHWELE (ki-)	G.32/*		Nghwele
ZARAMO (ki-)	G.33/*	ZARAMO:	Dzalamo
			DOE, DOHE
NGULU (ki-)	G.34/*	(NGURU):	
RUGURU (ki-)	G.35/*	⎰RUGURU	Luguru
KAMI (ki-)	G.36/o	⎱KAMI	
KUTU (ki-)	G.37/*		Khutu
VIDUNDA (ki-)	G.38/*		
SAGALA (ki-)	G.39/*	SAGARA:[1]	
		⎧ITUMBA	
		⎪KONDOA	Solwe
		⎪ZIRAHA	
		⎨KWENYI	
		⎪NKWIFIYA	
		⎩NKUNDA	

ZIGULA (ki-)

Where spoken: In the coastal area south of R. Pangani, nearly to 6° S., and inland for about 60 miles.
Number: 112,113.[2]
Classed with SHAMBALA by DB; the relationship is undoubtedly close.

DGHWELE (ki-)

Where spoken: In a narrow belt on the north bank of R. Wami.

ZARAMO (ki-)

Where spoken: In the coastal area, in the Bagamoyo–Dar-es-Salaam region, between R. Wami and 7° S., and inland to 37° 40' E.
Number: 173,518 (perhaps including DHWELE).
DOE or DOHE is the name of an offshoot of the ZARAMO on the Bagamoyo–Dar-es-Salaam District boundary.[3]
Number: 6,616.

NGULU (ki-)

Where spoken: In a narrow area 37° 30' E., 5°–6° 30' S.
Number: 65,672.
Considered as a dialect of ZIGULA by DB.

---

[1] List of dialects taken from Johnston.
[2] Figures for this Group from 1948 Census.
[3] A. Hartnoll, personal communication.

ZARAMO GROUP

RUGURU (ki-)

Where spoken: In Morogoro D.
Number: 179,078.
Considered as a dialect of ZARAMO by DB.

KAMI (ki-)

Where spoken: North-east of the Ruaha–Rufiji confluence.
Considered as a dialect of ZARAMO by DB.

KUTU (ki-)

Where spoken: North of R. Ruaha just above the Rufiji confluence, on the eastern edge of Morogoro D.
Number: 14,851.

VIDUNDA (ki-)

Where spoken: On the north bank of R. Ruaha, 37° E.
Number: 10,185.

SAGALA (ki-)

Where spoken: On the banks of R. Ruaha around Kilosa, 36° 20'–37° 20' E.
Number: 19,807.

According to DB SAGARA 'is used as the general term for a group of closely allied dialects'. He gives a list from Johnston (see above) in which, however, KAGURU is also included (see KAGULU in GOGO Group, p. 121).

TAITA GROUP[1]

Where spoken: K., T.T.

MG3		NBiii		Other names
TAITA	E.74:	TAITA		Teita
{DABIDA (ki-)	E.74a/*	{DABIDA (**ki-d'avida**)		Dabida
{SAGALA (ki-)	E.74b/*	{TERI		Sagalla
DIGO (ki-)	E.73/*	DIGO (ki-)		

But see NYIKA in SWAHILI Group, p. 129.

POKOMO (ki-)	E.71/*	POKOMO (ki-)	Pfokomo, Pokomo
NYIKA	E.72/*		

But see SWAHILI Group, p. 126.

†THARAKA
†CHUKA
See also KIKUYU
Group, p. 115.

TAITA (ki-)

Where spoken: K., west of Voi, 3° 25' S., 38° 20' E., extending into T.T.
Number: K. 48,561, T.T. 6,330.[2]
There are two dialects, which differ considerably:[3]

DABIDA (ki-), spoken in the northern part of the area, on Dabida massif and on parts of Sagalla massif. Local variants have been noted.

TERI (ki-), spoken on part of Sagalla massif.

DIGO (ki-)

Where spoken: K., T.T., in a coastal area south of the DURUMA.
Number: T.T. 32,144.
The DIGO are among the tribes generally recognized as NYIKA. It would appear, however, that their language differs from the NYIKA dialects (see p. 129).

POKOMO (ki-)

Where spoken: K., along the banks of R. Tana, from the equator to the sea, in an enclave among non-Bantu speakers.
Number: 16,355.
Used in primary education in initial stages.

NYIKA dialects—see SWAHILI Group, p. 126.

According to Lambert[4] THARAKA and the speech of the CHUKA stand between the KIKUYU and TAITA Groups. See KIKUYU Group, p. 115.

[1] Called NYIKA-TAITA in MG3.
[2] Figures for this Group from 1948 Census.
[3] Information from Mr. and Mrs. A. Harris, personal communication.
[4] Quoted in Middleton, *The Kikuyu and Kamba of Kenya*.

SWAHILI GROUP[1]

Where spoken: K., T.T., Zanzibar, Comoro Islands, &c.

Whiteley[2] and Bryan	MG3		Other names
SWAHILI:	SWAHILI	G.40:	Suaheli, Suahili, &c.
⎧MBALAZI (ci-)	⎧MBALAZI	G.41/o	
⎜BAJUNI	⎩TIKUU		Tikulu, Tukulu, Gunya
⎨PATE			Patta
⎜SIU			Siyu
⎩AMU	⎧AMU	G.42a/*	Lamu
MVITA	⎩MVITA	G.42b/*	
CIFUNDI (ci-)			
⎧VUMBA			
⎩MTADATA			
⎧PHEMBA	⎧PHEMBA	G.43a/*	Pemba
⎨TUMBATU	⎨TUMBATU	G.43b/*	
⎩HADIMU	⎩HADIMU	G.43c/*	
UNGUJA	⎧UNGUJA	G.42d/*	
'MRIMA'	⎩MRIMA	G.42c/*	
⎧NGAZIJA	⎧NGAZIJA	G.44a/*	Ngazidja
⎩NZWANI	⎩NJUANI	G.44b/o	Hinzua, Nzuani
NGWANA			Kingwana
'Bastard dialects'			
NYIKA:	NYIKA	E.72:	Nika, Nica, Nicat
⎧GIRYAMA	⎧GIRYAMA	E.72a/*	Giriama
⎜KAUMA	⎜KAUMA	E.72b/*	
⎨CONYI	⎨CONYI	E.72c/*	Chonyi, Dschogni
⎜DURUMA	⎜DURUMA	E.72d/*	
⎩RABAI	⎩RABAI	E.72e/*	
JIBANA			Dzihana
KAMBE			
RIBE			Rihe
? DIGO	DIGO	E.73/*	

See also TAITA Group, p. 125.

SWAHILI

Where spoken: (*a*) On the coast and islands:

On the Kenya and Tanganyika coast and islands from the Somalia border in the north to the P.E.A. border in the south. Farther north, it is spoken, or at least understood, in coastal areas of Somalia as far as Mogadishu, and to the south in P.E.A. as far as Mozambique. It is the language of Zanzibar and Pemba Islands, and dialects of SWAHILI are spoken in the Comoro Islands.

[1] The language prefix is **ki-** for all dialects of both Clusters except MBALAZI and CIFUNDI, where it is **ci-**.   [2] Personal communication.

SWAHILI GROUP

In the coastal regions of K. and T.T., SWAHILI is the mother-tongue in many areas (see below), and is also spoken fluently by those for whom it is not their mother tongue.

The main dialects of SWAHILI are:

MBALAZI, spoken by the AMARANI of Brava (Barawa) town in Somalia.[1]

BAJUNI, scattered along the coast and islands between Mogadishu and Zanzibar, but mainly north of Pate as far as Fuma and Kismayu.

The BAJUNI are called GUNYA by the Swahili and are also known as TIKUU ('from the big country').[2]

PATE, on Pate (Patta) Island.

SIU, on Siu Island.

AMU, on Lamu Island.

This is regarded as predominantly the language of poetry.

This group of northern dialects is characterized by having the -ile perfect form of the verb. PATE, SIU, and AMU are so closely similar that they are only classed here as separate dialects because they are considered as such by their speakers. The differences are mainly phonetic (H. E. Lambert).[3]

MVITA, on Mombasa Island (native name Mvita).

CIFUNDI, north of Vanga.

VUMBA, Wasin Island and Jimbo near Vanga; also on the mainland.[4]

MTADATA, between Pangani and Tanga; also said by local informants to be spoken around Sadani.

These two dialects are characterized by the presence of two separate sets of singular personal subject prefixes.

PHEMBA, on Pemba Island, except the southern tip.

TUMBATU, on Tumbatu Island north of Zanzibar, and on the southern tip of Pemba Island and the northern tip of Zanzibar Island.

HADIMU, in the southern part of Zanzibar Island.

These three dialects have post-radical harmony with the radical vowel of the verb.[5]

UNGUJA, in the central part of Zanzibar Island, especially in Zanzibar city.

The same dialect, with slight regional variations, is spoken on the mainland along the whole of the T.T. coast (except for pockets of other dialects noted above). On the mainland the dialect is known as MRIMA.

[1] V. L. Grottanelli, personal communication.
[2] TIKUU has long been known to be a SWAHILI dialect; Grottanelli confirms the suggestion originally made by Johnston that it is the same as BAJUNI.
[3] Personal communication.
[4] Lambert, 'The Vumba Verb' (*Bull. Interterritorial Language Committee*, 1953).
[5] Found also in VUMBA, in certain tenses.

UNGUJA is the dialect which forms the basis of present-day 'standard' SWAHILI, which is the language of education and literacy throughout the SWAHILI-speaking area. Within 'standard' SWAHILI there are variations, mainly of vocabulary, e.g. a higher proportion of words of Arabic origin in coastal and/or Moslem areas.

NGAZIJA, on Grand Comoro (Comoro Islands).[1]

NZWANI, on Anjouan (Johanna) (Comoro Islands).

The speech of Moheli Island (Comoro Islands) is known as ki-MWALI. It appears to be a NGAZIJA-NZWANI mixture. On Mayotte Island it is presumed that either NGAZIJA or NZWANI is spoken.

The Comoro dialects have post-radical harmony with the radical vowel of the verb in certain tenses, and appear also to have two sets of singular personal subject prefixes.

(b) Inland:

Tanganyika: SWAHILI is the language of administration and education throughout the Territory. 'Standard' SWAHILI, being sponsored by Government, is fairly uniform among people who have any contact with administrative or educational centres (Government or mission). Beyond that, however, the standard varies with individual speakers, the language being influenced to a greater or less degree by local languages, mainly in vocabulary and pronunciation. In some inland areas, notably Tabora, Ujiji and Mwanza, communities speaking SWAHILI as their mother tongue are to be found.

Kenya: It is the language of administration, but other languages have been recognized for use in education, and as alternatives in administration. In certain areas there is resistance to SWAHILI, especially in the GIKUYU (Bantu) and the LUO, MAASAI, NANDI, and KIPSIKIS (non-Bantu) areas.

Uganda: SWAHILI is fairly widely understood, especially in the northern (non-Bantu) areas, but is nowhere taught in schools. It is used as a medium of communication, e.g. in the police and P.W.D., and in hospitals, especially in tribally mixed areas.

Congo Belge: In many areas east of R. Congo, from Stanleyville in the north to Elisabethville in the south, SWAHILI is the basic means of communication, and is often known as ki-NGWANA. It is still used in administration, but is being progressively supplemented by French. In education its use or non-use is dependent on the policies of various missionary societies, some preferring 'standard' (Tanganyika) SWAHILI and others a more simplified form. In a few areas, notably Usumbura at the northern end of L. Tanganyika and Mambasa in the Ituri forest, communities speaking SWAHILI as their mother tongue are to be found.

'Bastard' dialects:

Various bastardized forms of SWAHILI are used, largely in Kenya but also elsewhere, e.g. the forms of speech known as:

ki-VITA, war-time, army SWAHILI (now beginning to die out).

ki-SETTLA, ki-SETTLER, as spoken by many European settlers, and understood by their domestic and farm staff. This nickname is fairly widely recognized.

[1] Information on the Comoro dialects from Heepe, *Die Komorendialekte Ngazidja, Nzwani und Mwali* (1920).

SWAHILI GROUP

ki-SHAMBA, up-country SWAHILI.
ki-HINDI, as spoken by Indians.

In addition, the nickname ki-BARA ('up-country') is used by coast-dwellers to denote the type of SWAHILI occurring in Government publications, especially the newspaper *Mambo Leo*, i.e. an uninspired and lifeless style. The nickname ki-GAVAMENTI or ki-SERIKALI is also sometimes used.

SWAHILI is accepted by the University of London for its Honours Degree in African studies. It is studied in schools and taken as a subject in the General Certificate of Education examination in Kenya, Tanganyika, Uganda, and Zanzibar.

SWAHILI has the most extensive vernacular literature of any Bantu language, including a considerable body of poetry going back to the eighteenth century (written in Arabic script) as well as much modern verse. Besides the large number of books (religious, educational, &c.) produced by Europeans there is now a growing amount of prose literature written by Africans. There are also about 60 SWAHILI newspapers and periodicals.

NYIKA (ki-)

Where spoken: K., in coastal areas immediately behind the SWAHILI coastal strip, for about 40 miles on each side of Malindi, and inland for about 60 miles.

Number: 39,125 (1948 Census).

The various dialects together known as NYIKA have generally been considered to belong to the TAITA Group, and are thus classified in MG3. There appear, however, to be considerable divergencies between these speeches. GIRYAMA shows such marked affinities with SWAHILI that it is here tentatively placed in this Group, together with the other NYIKA speeches. The fact that the DIGO have a special name (a-LUPANGA) for those NYIKA peoples who do not speak DIGO[1] suggests a linguistic difference reflected in MG's classification of DIGO as a separate unit from NYIKA. Tribally, however, the DIGO are considered as one of the nine NYIKA tribes. There is close relationship between the TAITA and SWAHILI Groups, and definitive classification is not possible without further research.

The nine tribes generally recognized as NYIKA,[2] and whose speeches are here considered as NYIKA, are:

GIRYAMA, from north of R. Sabaki to 10–15 miles inland from the upper Mleji stream; a few small settlements farther north.

KAUMA (*a*) on R. Sabaki (a few); (*b*) inland from Kilifi.

CONYI, near the KAUMA in both areas.

DURUMA, on both sides of the railway between Mazeras and Samburu stations, and south to 4° S.

RABAI, around Rabai.

JIBANA, adjacent to the KAMBE near Rabai.

KAMBE (*a*) on R. Sabaki; (*b*) near Rabai.

RIBE, near Rabai.

DIGO, south of the DURUMA on both sides of the K.–T.T. border.

[1] Prins, *The Coastal Tribes of the North-eastern Bantu* (Eth. Survey, 1952).
[2] Prins, op. cit.; Frank, *Habari na desturi za Waribe* (1953).

POGOLO GROUP

Where spoken: T.T.

MG3		*Other names*
POGOLO (ci-)	G.51/*	Pogoro
But see also HEHE	Group, p. 131.	
NDAMBA	G.52/0	

POGOLO (ci-)

Where spoken: Round Mahenge, roughly between R. Kilombero and R. Mbaragandu and southwards to 9° 30′ S.
Number: 63,187.[1]
Classed by DB in the 'Rufiji Group' (see HEHE Group, p. 131).

NDAMBA

Where spoken: On both banks of the middle Kilombero river, 36°–36° 30′ E.
Number: 19,032.

[1] Figures for this Group from 1948 Census.

(131)

HEHE GROUP

Where spoken: T.T.

MG3		DB	Other names
		'Rufiji Group':	
SANGO (eʃi-)	G.61/*	SANGO	Sangu, Rori
HEHE (eki-)	G.62/*	HEHE	
BENA (eki-)	G.63/*	BENA	
PANGWA (eki-)	G.64/*		
KJNGA (eki-)	G.65/*		
But see KINGA under NYAKYUSA, p. 79.			
WANJI	G.66/o		
KISI	G.67/o		Kisii
(MATUMBI (ki-)	P.13/*)	MATUMBI	
See NGINDO Group, p. 133.			
(POGOLO (ci-)	G.51/*)	POGORO	
See POGOLO Group, p. 130.			

SANGO (eʃi-)

Where spoken: North-east of Mbeya, 7° 30'–9° 30' S., 33° 30'–34° 50' E.
Number: 22,773.[1]

HEHE (eki-)

Where spoken: In a large area around Iringa, between R. Njombe and R. Kilombero, 34° 20'–37° E.
Number: 192,153.

BENA (eki-)

Where spoken: Round the headwaters of R. Kilombero, northwards to Sao hill and Kipengere, south to 9° S., extending from 36° 30' E. beyond Njombe in the west.
Number: 157,974.

PANGWA (eki-)

Where spoken: On the north-eastern shores of L. Nyasa.
Number: 37,680.

KJNGA (eki-)

Where spoken: In a small area near Njombe, 9° 10' S., 34° 40' E.
Number: 56,808.
Perhaps the KINGA grouped under NYAKYUSA by Tew[2] (see p. 79).

WANJI

Where spoken: Near Njombe, 9° 20' S., 34° 30' E.
Number: 17,932.

[1] Figures for this Group from 1948 Census.   [2] *Peoples of the Lake Nyasa Region.*

KISI

Where spoken: West of Njombe, 9° 20′ S., 34° 20′ E.

Number: 3,631 (erroneously named KISII in 1948 Census).

According to DB PANGWA is allied to SUTU and MATENGO (see MANDA Group, p. 136); he also adds to his 'Rufiji Group' POGORO and MATUMBI.

NGINDO GROUP[1]

Where spoken: T.T.

MG3		Other names
NDENGEREKO (ki-)	P.11/*	
RUIHI (ki-)	P.12/*	Rufiji
MATUMBI (ki-)	P.13/*	
But see also HEHE Group, p. 131.		
NGINDO (ki-)	P.14/*	
MBUNGA	P.15/*	
		KICHI (Hartnoll)[2]

NDENGEREKO (ki-)
Where spoken: (*a*) in Dar-es-Salaam D.; (*b*) in the Matumbi hills round Kibiti, Mchukivi, and Bungu.
Number: 53,307.[3]

RUIHI (ki-)
Where spoken: On both banks of R. Rufiji, from 38° E. to the coast, excluding the delta.
Number: 70,769.

MATUMBI (ki-)
Where spoken: In the Matumbi hills south of R. Rufiji.
Number: 40,631.
Classed by DB in the 'Rufiji Group'—see HEHE Group, p. 131.

NGINDO (ki-)
Where spoken: South of R. Rufiji, south-west of the RUIHI.
Number: 85,189.
DB considers it to belong to the YAO Group (see p. 134), but not on first-hand evidence.

MBUNGA
Where spoken: In the angle between Great Ruaha river and R. Rufiji.
Number: 10,034.

To this Group Hartnoll adds:
KICHI
Where spoken: West of the MATUMBI area.

---

[1] Called MATUMBI Group in MG3. The name used here is that of the language spoken by the largest number of people.
[2] Personal communication.   [3] Figures for this Group from 1948 Census.

YAO GROUP

Where spoken: T.T., P.E.A., N.

MG3		*Other names*
YAO (ci-)	P.21/*	Ayo, Djao, Adsawa, Adsoa, Ayawa, Achawa, Hiao, Hyao, Haiao, Veiao, Wajao, &c.
MWERA (ci-)	P.22/*	Mwela
MAKONDE (ci-)	P.23/*	Chinimakonde
NDONDE (ci-)	P.24/*	Kimawanda
MABIHA (ci-)	P.25/*	Mavia, Maviha, Mawia, Mawiha

YAO (ci-)

Where spoken: P.E.A., between R. Rovuma and R. Lujenda, nearly to L. Nyasa; across R. Rovuma into T.T., in a strip from Newala in the east to beyond Tunduru in the west; N., round the southern end of the lake, also near Blantyre, Chiradzulu, and Zomba, and in two small areas on the south-western shore of the lake.

Number: N. 281,177 (1945 Census), T.T. 126,741,[1] P.E.A. not known.

MWERA (ci-)

Where spoken: T.T., north of R. Lukuledi on the Rondo plateau.
Number: 126,412.

MAKONDE (ci-)

Where spoken: T.T., on the coast from south of Lindi to the mouth of R. Rovuma, and inland nearly to Masasi.
Number: 281,320.

NDONDE (ci-)

Where spoken: T.T., in the Newala area on the north bank of R. Rovuma.
Number: 12,120.

MABIHA (ci-)

Where spoken: P.E.A., on Mavia plateau south of R. Rovuma; also in T.T.
Number: Total *c.* 70,000 (Harries);[2] T.T. 13,286.

Classed as a MAKONDE dialect by DB; Tew[3] considers the MABIHA as part of the MAKONDE.

---

[1] Figures for this Group for T.T. from 1948 Census.
[2] 'Mawiha texts' (*Bantu St.*, 1940).
[3] Op. cit.

MAKUA GROUP

Where spoken: P.E.A., N., A. (also T.T.)

MG3		DB	Other names
MAKUA (i-)	P.31/*	MAKUA: ⎧MEDO ⎨ ⎩LOMWE	Makoa, Makoane, Makwa, Mato N. Makua
LOMWE (i-)	P.32/*		Lolo, Lomue, Cilowe, Nguru, W. Makua
NGULU (i-)	P.33/*		Nguru, Mihavane, Mihavani, Mihawani, W. Makua
CUABO (ci-)	P.34/o		Chuabo, Chwabo, Cuambo, Lolo

MAKUA (i-)
 Where spoken: P.E.A., in a large area south of R. Lujenda; also to the north in T.T.
 Number: T.T. 95,464 (1948 Census).
 Used in primary education.
 DB distinguishes two dialects: MEDO and LOMWE (but see below).

LOMWE (i-)
 Where spoken: P.E.A., south of R. Lurio, reaching nearly to the coast in the south.

NGULU (i-)
 Where spoken: P.E.A. and N., along the upper Lurio river.
 Number: N. 379,638 (1945 Census).
 According to Tew[1] NGURU is an old name for the people of the region, now particularly applied to the LOMWE in Nyasaland.
 Tew describes the MIHAVANI as a MARAVI-LOMWE mixture, between Mrupa and Marata hills to the south and Mrietu to the east.

CUABO (ci-)
 Where spoken: P.E.A., between Quelimane and the Mlanje mountains.
 The CUABO are considered as part of the LOMWE by Tew, as are also the PODZO (but see NSENGA Group, p. 141).

[1] *Peoples of the Lake Nyasa Region.*

MANDA GROUP

Where spoken: T.T., N.

MG3		Chale[1]	Other names
MANDA (ci-)	N.11/*	MANDA (ki-) ⎫	Nyasa
MPOTO (ci-)	N.14/*	MPOTO (ki-) ⎭	
MATENGO (ci-)	N.13/*	MATENGO (ki-)	
†NGONI (ci-)	N.13/*	NGONI (ki-) = SUTU (ki-)	
See also NGUNI Group, p. 152.			
TONGA (ci-)	N.15/*	TONGA (ki-)	Siska, Sisya, W. Nyasa

See also TUMBUKA Group, p. 137.

MANDA (ki-)
Where spoken: On the north-eastern shore of L. Nyasa, 10° 20′ S.

MPOTO (ki-)
Where spoken: On the eastern shore of L. Nyasa from Manda to the P.E.A. border.

According to Chale MANDA and MPOTO are very similar; both are also loosely known as NYASA (ki-).

MATENGO (ki-)
Where spoken: In a narrow strip inland from L. Nyasa, and eastwards to the upper Rovuma river, 10° 20′–11° 30′ S.

Number: 57,637.[2]

DB refers to SUTU, with dialect MATENGO (but see below); he states that PANGWA (see HEHE Group, p. 131) is allied to SUTU.

†NGONI (SUTU) (ki-)
Where spoken: In a large area round Songea, as far as 9° 20′ S.; 35° 20′–37 ° E.

Number: 102,994.

According to DSB 'while retaining typical Zulu vocabulary and morphology, particularly that of the verb, [NGONI] has acquired much from Eastern Bantu'. He is, however, citing a 1904 source,[3] and MG[4] states that the language as now spoken is unquestionably closely related to TONGA, though still with some NGUNI elements. Chale describes it as based on the original language of the SUTU people, with some additions from neighbouring languages (MANDA, MATENGO, &c.), as well as ZULU elements.

TONGA (ci-)
Where spoken: N., on the western shore of L. Nyasa, 11°–12° S.

Number: 50,359.

Classed by DB with TUMBUKA in the 'Nyasa Group'; Tew[5] lists TONGA among the TUMBUKA tribes; she lists SISKA as a separate tribe, north of the TONGA.

---

[1] Sebastian Chale (a m-MANDA), personal communication.
[2] Figures for this Group from 1948 Census (T.T.) and 1945 Census (N.).
[3] Spiss, 'Kingoni und Kisutu' (*M.S.O.S.*, 1904).
[4] Personal communication.   [5] Op. cit.

TUMBUKA SINGLE UNIT

Where spoken: T.N., T., N.R.

MG3		Tew (Tribes)[1]	Other names
TUMBUKA	N.21:	TUMBUKA:	Tambuka, Timbuka, Tumboka
TUMBUKA (ci-)	N.21/*[2]	TUMBUKA	Tombucas
KAMANGA (ci-)	N.21/*	KAMANGA	Henga
		HENGA	
(TONGA (ci-)	N.21/*)	TONGA	
See MANDA Group, p. 136.			
		SISYA	Siska
		KANDAWIRE	
		FULILWA	Fulirwa
		NTHALI	
		HEWE	Hewa
POKA (ci-)	N.21/*	PHOKA	
YOMBE	N.21/o		
SENGA	N.21/o		
		Non-TUMBUKA:	
FUNGWE	N.21/o	FUNGWE	
WENYA	N.21/o	WENYA	
		NYIKA	
(TAMBO	N.21/o)	TAMBO	Tembo
See NYIHA-SAFWA Group, p. 77.			
LAMBIA	N.27/o		LAMBYA, Lambwa
See NYIHA-SAFWA Group.			

TUMBUKA (ci-)
Where spoken: N., N.R., north of R. Dwangwa, south of the North Rukuru river, between L. Nyasa in the east and the Luangwa valley in the west.
Number: c. 156,000 (1934 Census, N.R.—1945 Census, N.).
Used in primary education.

MG1 lists a number of dialects; Tew a number of tribal sections:

TUMBUKA, in the lower South Rukuru and Kasitu valleys.

KAMANGA, on the north bank of the lower South Rukuru and its tributaries the Luviri and Runyima, and into N.R.

HENGA (considered by MG1 as an alternative name for KAMANGA), in the plain at the mouth of the South Rukuru river, and on R. Luviri and North Rukuru river.

TONGA, classed in the MANDA Group by MG3 (see p. 136). According to Tew, the TONGA do not consider themselves to be TUMBUKA, but are linguistically akin.

[1] Op. cit. [2] List of dialects from MG1.

SISYA (SISKA, an alternative name for TONGA, according to MG3), between the Choma mountains and L. Nyasa.

KANDAWIRE, round Mt. Waller and to the north.

FULILWA, north of Florence Bay.

NTHALI and HEWE, on the Nyika plateau.

POKA, east of the Nyika plateau.

YOMBE, round Chekamgombe hill.

SENGA, on both banks of the upper Luangwa river, 10° 30'–12° S. A TUMBUKA-ized BISA offshoot.[1]

Number: c. 23,000 (Whiteley).

FUNGWE, north of the YOMBE.

WENYA.

NYIKA.

TAMBO (classed by MG3 in the NYIHA-SAFWA Group, p. 77).

LAMBYA (ici-) See NYIHA-SAFWA Group.

There is considerable SWAZI influence in the TUMBUKA dialects, according to MG.[2]

[1] Whiteley, *Bemba and Related Peoples of Northern Rhodesia*.
[2] Personal communication.

(139)

NYANJA SINGLE UNIT

Where spoken: N., N.R., P.E.A.

MG3		Tew (Tribes)[1]	Other names
		MARAVI:	Marave, Malawi
NYANJA (ci-)	N.31:	⎧NYANJA:	Chinyanja
⎧NYANJA (ci-)	N.31a/*	⎧NYANJA	
⎪		⎨NYASA	
⎨MADANJA (ci-)	N.31c/*	⎩MANG'ANJA	Maganja, Mangandja, Waganga, Nyungwe, Sena
⎪			
⎩CEWA (ci-)	N.31b/*	CEWA	Chewa, Chewa, Cheva, Sheva
			PETA (DB), Cipeta, Maravi
(NSENGA (ci-)	N.41/*)	NSENGA	
See NSENGA Group, p. 141.			
MBO	(MG1, N.32/o)	(A)MBO	
		TONGA	
		MAKANGA	
		TUMBA	
		MATENGO	
		See HEHE and MANDA Groups, pp. 131, 136.	
MAZARO	(MG1, N.33/o)		

Note: Atkins[2] considers SENA and NYUNGWE to belong to this Group (see NSENGA Group, p. 141).

NYANJA (ci-)

Where spoken: N. (*a*) inland from L. Nyasa to the N.R. border, 12° 10′–13° 50′ E., and on the eastern shore for about 70 miles; (*b*) on the upper Shire river, south to Blantyre and L. Shirwa.

Number: 312,482 (1945 Census).

The unified standard literary form, which is used in administration and education, particularly in southern Nyasaland, is based on MADANJA, CEWA, and PETA (DB). The Bible has been published in a 'Union' version.

Tew distinguishes between:

NYANJA, on the southern shore of the lake;

NYASA, on the eastern shore, north to the Matengo mountains (including a settlement of freed slaves at Masasi in T.T.), south to the YAO country.

DB distinguishes 'a closely allied form, differing somewhat', spoken on the eastern shore of the lake, from the mission centre on Likoma Island.

[1] *Peoples of the Lake Nyasa Region.* [2] Personal communication.

NYANJA SINGLE UNIT

MADANJA (ci-)

Where spoken: N., on the lower Shire and Zambezi rivers, and across into Tete D. (where the people are known as NYUNGWE) and Sena D. (where they are known as SENA) (Tew). See, however, NYUNGWE and SENA in NSENGA Group, p. 141.

CEWA (ci-)

Where spoken: N., N.R., P.E.A., at the junction of the three territories, between R. Zambezi in the south, R. Luangwa in the north, and the southern end of L. Nyasa in the east.

Number: N. 576,143 (1945 Census), N.R. *c.* 77,000 (Tew).[1]

DB distinguishes as a separate dialect:

> PETA, 'the western form' of NYANJA. This dialect is also spoken by many NGONI who have lost their own language, and is called by them ci-NGONI (MG).[2]

Tew adds the names of several small groups of people 'usually classed with Cewa or Nyanja':

(A)MBO, south of R. Ruo and on the Kirk range. Perhaps a sub-branch of the MARAVI or an offshoot of the AMBO of the Luangwa valley.

MG1 includes MBO in the NYANJA Group (from Johnston). He was, however, unable to find any trace of the MBO language.[2]

TONGA of the lower Shire. Perhaps immigrant Zambezi TONGA.

TUMBA, near the upper Shire.

MATENGO. But see HEHE and MANDA Groups, pp. 131, 136.

MG1 also adds MAZARO, from Johnston. He was, however, unable to find any trace of this language.[2] Mazaro is marked on maps as a place-name on the lower Zambezi.

[1] Quoting Orde Browne, 1938.   [2] Personal communication.

NSENGA GROUP[1]

Where spoken: N.R., S.R., P.E.A.

MG3		Other names
NSENGA (ci-)	N.41/*	Senga
KUNDA (ci-)	N.42/*	Chikunda, Cikunda
NYUNGWE (ci-)	N.43/*	Teta
SENA (ci-)	N.44/*	
		TONGA (DB)
RUE (ci-)	N.45/o	
PODZO (ci-)	N.46/o	

NSENGA (ci-)

Where spoken: N.R., on the Zambezi–Luangwa watershed plateau.
Number: +45,000 (Tew).[2]
Used in sub-standard education.
The NSENGA are placed by Tew among the MARAVI tribes (see NYANJA Group, p. 139).

KUNDA (ci-)

Where spoken: P.E.A. and adjoining parts of N. and N.R. (*a*) on both banks of R. Zambezi from the Luangwa confluence to 32° E.; (*b*) on the east bank of R. Luangwa, 13°–14° S.
Number: N. 72,866 (1945 Census), N.R. 27,000 (1934 Census).
Classed as a dialect of SENA by DB.

NYUNGWE (ci-)

Where spoken: P.E.A., on both banks of R. Zambezi, 33°–34° E.
Classed as a dialect of SENA by DB. According to Tew NYUNGWE is the name of a part of the MANG'ANJA (see NYANJA Group, p. 139).

SENA (ci-)

Where spoken: P.E.A., on both banks of the Zambezi around Sena and Shumba, and northwards to Port Herald on the lower Shire.
According to Tew SENA is the name of a part of the MANG'ANJA.

DB considers KUNDA, NYUNGWE, and RUE to be SENA dialects, and adds TONGA. Atkins[3] classes SENA and NYUNGWE in the NYANJA Group (see p. 139).

---

[1] Called SENGA-SENA Group in MG3. The name used here is that of the best-known unit of the Group; the spelling NSENGA is preferred, partly to avoid confusion with SENGA (see TUMBUKA, p. 137).
[2] Op. cit.
[3] Personal communication.

RUE (ci-)

Where spoken: P.E.A., S.R., 16° 20′–19° 20′ S., 33°–35° E.
Classed as a SENA dialect by DB; it appears to be very little known.

PODZO (ci-)

Where spoken: P.E.A., on the coast at the Zambezi delta from just north of Beira almost to Quelimane, and for over 100 miles inland.
Number: 4,588 (Tew).[1]
According to Tew the PODZO are related to the LOMWE (see MAKUA Group, p. 135).

[1] Quoting Junod, 1936.

SHONA GROUP[1]

Where spoken: S.R., P.E.A.

DSB	MG3		EW, *and other names*
	KOREKORE	S.11:	N. Shona, Chishona
⎧TAVARA	⎧TABARA	S.11c/o	
⎪	⎪SHANGWE	S.11a/o	Shaŋwe (O)
⎪KOREKORE:	⎩KOREKORE	S.11b/*	
⎨ ⎧Urungwe			
⎪ ⎪Sipolilo			
⎪ ⎨TANDE			
⎪ ⎪NYONGWE			
⎪ ⎩PFUNDE			
⎪GOVA (see also below)			GOBA (EW); Goʋa (O)
⎩BUDYA	BUDYA	S.11d/o	BUDYA (EW); Ɓudya (O)
ZEZURU:	ZEZURU	S.12/*	C. Shona, Chiswina, Chishona
⎧ ⎧SHAWASHA			
⎪ ⎪GOVA (see also above)			
⎪ ⎨MBIRE			
⎪ ⎪KWACHIKWAKWA			Ʋakwacikwakwa (O), Cikwakwa
⎪ ⎩TSUNGA			Tsuŋga (O)
⎨HARAVA			HARABA (EW); Haraʋa (O)
⎪NOHWE			
⎪NJANJA			
⎪NOBVU			
⎪KWAZWIMBA,			ZIMBA (EW);
⎩ KWAZVIMBA (N)			Ʋakwazimba (O)
KARANGA:	KARANGA	S.14/*	Karaŋa (O)
⎧ ⎧GOVERA			GOBERA (EW); Goʋera (O)
⎪ ⎪NGOVA			NGOBA (EW); (D)goʋa (O)
⎨ ⎨DUMA			'DUMA (EW); Ɗuma (O)
⎪ ⎩JENA			
⎪ ⎧MHARI			Mari
⎩ ⎩NYUBI			NYU'BI (EW); Nyuɓi (O)

[1] In the first column the new (1956) orthography, where different from DSB, is indicated by (N); in the third column Westphal's spelling is given in capitals, and the old orthography, instituted by Doke, is indicated by (O).

The language prefix is ci- (new orthography chi-) throughout.

SHONA GROUP

MANYIKA:	MANYIKA	S.13:	
⎧HUNGWE			
⎪MANYIKA:	⎧MANYIKA	S.13a/*	
⎪ ⎧UNYAMA			
⎪ ⎪KAROMBE			
⎪ ⎪BUNJI			'BUNJI (EW); Ɓunji (O)
⎨ ⎨NYAMUKA	⎨		
⎪ ⎪DOMBA			'DOMBA (EW); Ɗomba (O)
⎪ ⎪NYATWE			
⎪ ⎪GUTA			
⎪ ⎪HERE			
⎪ ⎪BVUMBA			
⎪ ⎪JINDWI			
⎪ ⎩BOCA			'BOCA (EW); Ɓoca (O)
⎩TEVE	⎩TEƁE	S.13b/o	Teʋe (O)
NDAU:	NDAU	S.15/*	SE. Shona, Sofala
⎧ ⎧NDAU			
⎪ ⎩TONGA			
⎨GARWE			
⎪DANDA			
⎩SHANGA			
KALANGA:	KALAƊA	S.16/*	Kalaŋga (O), Kalana, W. Shona
⎧ROZWI, ROZVI (N)			Roʑi (O)
⎪ ⎧NYAI			
⎪ ⎩NAMBZYA			
⎨KALANGA			Kalaka
⎪LILIMA			Humbe
⎪ ⎧PERI			
⎩ ⎩TALAHUNDRA			
			†BIRWA (EW). See also SOTHO Group, p. 148.

Number: −1,000,000 (DSB).

The name SHONA is a generic name for speakers of all the units in this Group, used by the people themselves as well as by outsiders (the name was originally that used by the NDEBELE). SWINA, a name found in older literature, is regarded as derogatory, and is no longer used (Tucker).[1]

Proposals for a unified orthography, with unification of the language over a wide area, were accepted in 1929, and since then the Bible has been published in 'Union SHONA', and there is a growing volume of vernacular literature. KALANGA was excluded from the unification as being too divergent from the other SHONA speeches.

[1] Personal communication.

SHONA GROUP

KOREKORE[1]

Where spoken: S.R. (and P.E.A.), in a broad belt south of the Zambezi from 20° almost to 33° E.

Dialects:

TABARA, in Darwin D., in the eastern part of Chimanda Reserve.

SHANGWE, in Shangwe D. and in Lower Gwelo and Que Que Reserves.

KOREKORE, with variants (see list above), in Lomagundi and Darwin Districts, also in Mrewa and Mazoe Districts.

GOBA, spoken by riverine people in Urungwe and the north-eastern part of Sebungwe.

'BUDYA, in Mtoko D., also in Mrewa and Mazoe Districts.

ZEZURU

Where spoken: S.R., in the Salisbury area, westward to Gatooma, south to the foothills of the Udzi mountains, east to Nyinga on the P.E.A. border, north to the town of Mount Darwin.

For dialects, see list above.

KARANGA

Where spoken: S.R., around Fort Victoria–Zimbabwe.

Dialects:

GOBERA, in Gutu, Chilimanzi and Victoria Districts.

NGOBA, in Selukwe D.

'DUMA, in Victoria and Ndanga Districts.

JENA, in Victoria and Ndanga Districts.

The above dialects 'constitute typical Karanga' (DSB).

MHARI, in Chibi D.

NYU'BI, in Selukwe D.

The above dialects are 'extreme types' (DSB).

MANYIKA

Where spoken: S.R., mainly in Umtali, Inyanga, and Marandellas Districts; also in P.E.A.

For dialects, see list above.

NDAU

Where spoken: P.E.A., S.R., in an area bounded by the Beira–Umtali railway in the north, the coast in the west, and R. Save in the south.

For dialects, see list above.

KALANGA

Where spoken: S.R. (*a*) south-west of Bulawayo (KALANGA and LILIMA); (*b*) south of the Zambezi on both sides of the Shangani confluence (ROZVI); (*c*) in a

[1] The new orthography is used for the major units of this Group.

small area round Gwaai, between Bulawayo and R. Limpopo (NYAI and NAMBZYA; some NAMBZYA, however, live at L. Ngami).

Dialectal differences are not great.

†BIRWA

Where spoken: British Bechuanaland and north-western Transvaal.

A mixed language, standing between the SHONA and SOTHO Groups.

VENDA SINGLE UNIT

Where spoken: S.A., also in S.R.

	MG3		*Other names*
	VEṆḌA (cẹ-)	S.21/*	Venda (tshi-)

Where spoken: On the middle Limpopo river, mainly on the south bank, between Louis Trichardt and the Game Reserve.

Used in primary education and religious instruction.

Dialectal differences are not great; DSB names two dialects PHANI and TAVHA-TSINDI, on which the 'literary' language is based.

SOTHO-TSWANA GROUP

Where spoken: B.P., S.A., Basutoland

EW based on DSB	Official orthography	MG3		Other names
SUTHU (Southern):	SOTHO (se-)	SOTHO (se-)	S.32*	Suto, Sesuto
⎰TAUŊ	TAUNG			
⎱†PHUTHI				
See NGUNI Group, p. 152.				
TSWANA:	TSWANA	TSWANA (se-)	S.31:	Chuana, Cuana, Coana, Tšwana
⎰ŊWATU	NGWATO	⎰ŊWATU	S.31c/o	Mangwato
⎱TAWANA	TAWANA			
⎰KXHATLA	KGATLA	⎱KGATLA	S.31b/o	
⎱KHATLA	KHATLA			
KWENA	KWENA			Koena
ŊWAKETSI	NGWAKETSE			
⎰HURUTSI	HURUTSHE			
⎱ROLOŊ	ROLONG	⎱ROLOŊ	S.31a/*	
⎰THLARU (tɬharu)	THLARO			
⎱THLAPIŊ (tɬhapiŋ)	THLAPING			Tlapi
KXALAXARI	KGALAGADI			Khalahadi
LETE				
†BIRWA				
See also SHONA Group, p. 143.				
PEDI (N. SUTHU):	PEDI (se-)	PEDI (se)	S.32b/*	N. Sotho, Transvaal Sotho
⎧PEDI				
⎪⎰MASEMULA	MASEMOLA			
⎪⎱KXAXA	KGAGA			
⎪KONI				
⎨ TSWENI	TSWENE			
⎪KWENA				
⎪ (See also under TSWANA above)				
⎪XANANWA	GANANWA			
⎪⎰PULANA	PULANA			
⎩⎱PHALABURWA (thi-)	PHALA-BORWA			

SOTHO-TSWANA GROUP

EW based on DSB	Official orthography	MG3		Other names
KHUTSWI	KHUTSWE	KHUTSHWE	S.32c/o	Kutswe
LUBEDU (khi-) PHALABURWA	LOBEDU	LOBEDU	S.32a/*	Lovedu
DOGWA	TLOKWA			Tokwa, Tlokoa
†PAI		PAI	S.32d/*	Mbai, Mbayi
See also NGUNI Group, p. 152.				
†NREBELE				
See NGUNI Group.				
†NDZUNDZA				
See NGUNI Group.				
LOZI (si-)		(LOZI	K.21/*)	
See also LUYANA Group, p. 70.				

Four languages are recognized for educational and literary purposes, each of which serves for speakers of more or less closely related languages and dialects. The units of this Group are therefore classed under the languages which serve them.

SOTHO (i.e. S. SUTHU, TSWANA, or N. SUTHU) is accepted by the University of London for its Honours Degree in African studies.

Southern SOTHO

Where spoken: Basutoland and parts of O.F.S., the south-eastern Transvaal, and by a few speakers in Natal; also in industrial and mining areas of Witwatersrand, Pretoria, and Bloemfontein.

Number of speakers: c. 3,000,000 (DSB).

There is a growing body of literature, including 'vernacular works of no mean merit' (DSB).

'There are no distinctive dialectal types of Southern Sotho' (DSB).

It is also spoken, with slight variations, by the TLOKWA now in north-eastern Barotseland; Tucker[1] notes a variant:

TAUD, spoken in Basutoland, around Mohale's Hoek, and into O.F.S.

†PHUTHI is a mixed language—see NGUNI Group, p. 152.

TSWANA

Where spoken: Western and central Transvaal; the northern part of Cape Province (Bechuanaland); O.F.S., especially in the east and north-west, extending into B.P.; there are offshoots in Plumtree (S.R.), and in the Epukiro Reserve (S.W.A.).

Number of speakers: c. 852,000 (Schapera).[2]

There is a considerable body of vernacular literature.

TSWANA serves for speakers of:

DWATU, in B.P. in a roughly triangular area, Francistown–Serowe–Makarikari Pans; also spoken by:

TAWANA, a DWATU subsection in southern Ngamiland, in the Okavango delta.

[1] Personal communication. [2] *The Tswana* (Eth. Survey, 1953).

SOTHO-TSWANA GROUP

KXATLA, in western Transvaal, centred on Rustenberg; also spoken by:
KHATLA, in B.P., in the Bakhatla Reserve; and by
TLOKWA remnants from the eastern O.F.S. and Basutoland.

KWENA, in B.P., Bakwena Reserve, and in western areas of Transvaal north of Rustenberg.

ŊWAKETSI, in B.P., Bangwaketse Reserve.

HURUTSI, in western Transvaal and the adjacent corner of Cape Province south of R. Molopo.

ROLOŊ, in south-western Transvaal and northern O.F.S.; a small group on and around Thabanchu hill east of Bloemfontein; also in Cape Province (Bechuanaland).

THLARU, in Cape Province, in the Mafeking-Vryburg-Kuruman area.
One of the forms used for publications (DSB).

THLAPIŊ, in Cape Province, in the Taung-Vryburg-Kuruman-Barkly West-Douglas area.
Until recently, literary work was mainly based on this dialect (DSB).

KXALAXARI, in B.P., scattered between Lehututu and L. Ngami.
According to DSB 'an extreme dialectal connexion ... sufficiently different from Tswana to warrant a separate classification, but more information is necessary before this can be done satisfactorily'.

DSB adds LETE as a TSWANA dialect.

†BIRWA, a mixed language, spoken on the B.P.-Transvaal border east of Serowe, centred on Bobonong. See also SHONA Group, p. 143.

PEDI (Northern SOTHO)

Where spoken: Transvaal, in the Pietersburg-Middleburg-Lydenburg-Letaba area; also in the Blaawberg area.
There is a considerable body of vernacular literature.

Northern SOTHO serves for speakers of:
PEDI, around Johannesburg.
Number: Estimated at 500,000 (Jacottet, 1940).
The dialect on which 'literary' Northern SOTHO is based.
Also spoken by:
MASEMULA (NGUNI refugees), around Middleburg.
KXAXA, south of Pietersburg, including:
KONI and TSWENI.
A few KWENA east of Potgietersrust (but see under TSWANA).

XANANWA, in the Blaawberg area north of Pietersburg.

PULANA (thi-), in the low veldt east of R. Lebombo between Bushbuck Ridge and R. Olifants, south of the river adjoining the Game Reserve.
Also spoken by some PHALABURWA north of R. Olifants (who call their speech NARI; their own dialect is virtually extinct).

SOTHO-TSWANA GROUP

KHUTSWI, south of the PULANA between Graskop and Sabi in the Game Reserve.
This dialect is strongly influenced by NGUNI.

LUBEDU (khi-), in the Lobedu Reserve and adjacent areas east of Duivelskloof. Also spoken by some PHALABURWA (see also under PULANA).

DOGWA (TLOKWA).

†PAI, in eastern Transvaal, in the Nelspruit area.
This dialect, which is still spoken by old people, but is not likely to survive long (DSB), is a mixture of PEDI, or perhaps PULANA, and SWAZI. It is classed with SOTHO by DSB, but according to EW is probably closer to NGUNI (see NGUNI Group, p. 152).

†NREBELE, in central Transvaal. See NGUNI Group.

†NDZUNDZA, north of Pretoria. A mixture of NREBELE and PEDI. See NGUNI Group.

†LOZI (si-)

Where spoken: N.R. and Bechuanaland (*a*) on the east bank of R. Zambezi from just north of Luena to the R. Lui confluence, and inland for about 40 miles; (*b*) in a small enclave 17° 10′ S., 27° 20′ E.

Number: N.R. 67,193 (1934 Census).

The original language of the KOLOLO conquerors of the LOZI in the nineteenth century was SOTHO, and the present LOZI language is a mixture of SOTHO and LUYI. See LUYANA Group, p. 70.

NGUNI GROUP

Where spoken: S.A., also S.R. and N.R.

EW based on DSB	MG3		Other names
ZULU:			
⎧ ZULU (isi-)	ZULU	S.42a/*	Zunda
⎪ ⎧ of Zululand			
⎨ ⎨ of Natal			
⎪ ⎪ LALA			
⎪ ⎩ QWABE			
⎪ NDE'BELE (isi-ndeɓele)	NDEBELE	S.44/*	Tabele, Tebele
⎩ NGONI (Nyasaland)	NGONI	S.42b/*	Nguni
XHOSA (isi-):	XHOSA	S.41/*	Xosa, Kaffer, Kaffir
⎧ GCALEKA (isi-g̶/aleka)			
⎪ NDLAMBE (isi-nǰambe)			
⎪ GAIKA (isi-ŋg!ika)			Ncqika
⎨ THEMBU			
⎪ BOMVANA			
⎪ MPONDOMSE (isi-mpondomisi)			Mpondomisi
⎪ MPONDO			
⎩ XESIBE (isi-//esibe)			
SWATI (SWAZI) (isi-)	SWATI	S.43/*	Tekela, Tekeza
⎧ 'BACA (isi-ɓa/a)			
⎨ HLUBI (isi-ɬubi)			
⎩ †PHUTHI			
See also SOTHO-TSWANA Group, p. 148.			
†PAI̧			
See also SOTHO-TSWANA Group.			
†NREBELE			
See also SOTHO-TSWANA Group.			
†NDZUNDZA			
See also SOTHO-TSWANA Group.			
'Kitchen KAFFIR'			isi-Piki, isi-Lololo, Fanekalo, Fanakalo
'Old MFENGU' (extinct)			Fingo

NGUNI (i.e. ZULU or XHOSA) is accepted by the University of London for its Honours Degree in African studies.

ZULU (isi-)

Where spoken: Zululand and Natal, and in adjoining parts of south-eastern Transvaal and north-eastern O.F.S.; also in industrial centres.

There is a considerable body of vernacular literature.

There are no dialectal differences of any importance, but DSB distinguishes:

    'ZULU proper'; standard ZULU is based on the dialects of Zululand and Natal. LALA and QWABE, in Zululand.

NGUNI GROUP

NDE'BELE (isi-)

Where spoken: S.R., round Bulawayo and in the Matopos hills.

Used in primary education and religious instruction. It has been developed considerably as a separate literary language from standard ZULU, with a different orthography.

NGONI

Where spoken: N., north of Kasungu.

This speech is fairly close to ZULU (Atkins).[1]

Note: The NGONI of N.R. probably speak NYANJA languages (see NYANJA Group, p. 139) (Atkins). The NGONI of T.T. speak a language of the MANDA Group (see p. 136) (MG1).

XHOSA (isi-)

Where spoken: S.A., Cape Province, Ciskei, and Transkei, as far as the Natal border.

Number: +2,500,000 (DSB).

There is a considerable body of vernacular literature.

Dialectal differences would appear to be slight. DSB distinguishes the following:
  GCALEKA, NDLAMBE, GAIKA. 'Literary' XHOSA is based on these dialects.

  THEMBU, BOMVANA, MPONDOMSE.

  MPONDO, in Pondoland. This dialect diverges considerably from standard XHOSA.

  XESIBE. Has some affinities with SWAZI.

SWATI (isi-swati)

Where spoken: Swaziland and adjoining areas to the north and west.

Number: +250,000 (DSB).

Not used in education, ZULU being used instead.

DSB includes in his TEKEZA Group (i.e. SWAZI) some languages related to SWAZI but influenced to a greater or lesser degree by other languages:

'BACA

Where spoken: Southern Natal on the Cape Province border.

Strongly influenced by ZULU.

HLUBI

Where spoken: Southern Basutoland and adjoining areas in Cape Province.

Influenced by XHOSA.

†PHUTHI

Where spoken: Eastern Cape Province in East Griqualand, and across the border into southern Basutoland.

'... an extreme form of Nguni ... with strong Sotho influence' (DSB). See also SOTHO-TSWANA Group, p. 148.

[1] Personal communication.

NGUNI GROUP

The following are mixed languages or dialects, consisting of SOTHO and NGUNI elements:

†PAI̯, a mixture of SWAZI and PEDI̯, or perhaps PU̯LANA (see p. 151).

†NREḆELE, spoken by ancient NGUNI settlers in central Transvaal, between Middleburg and Pretoria and between Pretoria and Potgietersrust. There are two main dialects, spoken around Middelburg and Potgietersrust respectively.

†NDZUNDZA, spoken south of Pretoria. A mixture of NREḆELE and PEDI̯.

A pidgin language, 'Kitchen KAFFIR', is spoken over a wide area, from Durban to Witwatersrand, from the Copperbelt to East London, by Europeans and by African men (women are usually not fluent). It is also known as isi-PIKI, isi-LOLOLO, and the same or another pidgin is called FANEKALO or FANAKALO. 'Kitchen KAFFIR' owes a large portion of its vocabulary to ZULU and XHOSA, with English and Afrikaans admixture.

'Old MFENGU', now extinct, but known from older writers, belonged to the NGUNI Group.

TSONGA GROUP

Where spoken: S.R., P.E.A., S.A.

EW based on DSB	MG3		Other names
RONGA (ʃi-)	RONGA	S.54/*	
KONDE			
	GWAMBA	S.52/*	
TSONGA (ʃi-tsoŋga):	TSONGA	S.53:	Thonga, Tonga, Shangaan
⎧ TSONGA (GWAMBA)	⎧ TSONGA	S.53b/o	Gwapa
⎪ JONGA (djoŋga)	⎪ JONGA	S.53c/o	Djonga
⎨ HLANGANU (ʃi-ɬaŋganu)	⎨ HLANGANU	S.53a/*	Shangaan
⎪ NGWALUNGU (ʃi-ŋwaluŋgu)	⎪		
⎩ BILA (vila)	⎩ BILA	S.53d/o	
	TSWA	S.51:	
⎧ HLENGWE (ʃi-ɬeŋgwe)	⎧ HLENGWE	S.51a/o	
⎪ ⎧ MAKWAKWE	⎪		
⎨ ⎩ KHAMBANA	⎨		
⎪ TSWA (ʃi-)	⎪		
⎪ ⎧ DZIBI	⎩ TSWA	S.51b/*	Sheetswa
⎩ ⎩ DZONGA			

'The name Tsonga has been accepted as a term of reference for the whole group' (DSB).

Total number of speakers: —1,250,000 (DSB).

RONGA (ʃi-)

Where spoken: P.E.A., S.A., in a coastal belt about 40 miles wide, south of Lourenço Marques to 27° 30′ S.
Used in religious teaching.
DSB describes KONDE as 'a southern dialect influenced by Zulu'.

GWAMBA is classed by MG3 as a separate unit in this Group. But see under TSONGA below.

TSONGA (ʃi-)
DSB distinguishes the following dialects:
GWAMBA

Where spoken: S.A., mainly in Transvaal, extending into P.E.A.
DSB describes GWAMBA as 'the principal dialect [of TSONGA] ... built up of elements of the other four dialects of this Cluster, with accretions from Ronga'.
MG3 distinguishes between GWAMBA, which he classes as a separate unit in the Group, and the TSONGA dialect of the TSONGA Cluster. On the map in MG1 GWAMBA is shown north of TSONGA.

TSONGA GROUP

JONGA
Where spoken: On the coast north of Lourenço Marques, extending north-eastwards to R. Limpopo.

HLANGANU (ʃi-)
Where spoken: Around Lydenburg, extending north-eastwards to the P.E.A. border.

NGWALUNGU (ʃi-) (no location given in DSB).

ḄILA
Where spoken: On the coast immediately west of the Limpopo estuary.

HLENGWE (ʃi-)
Where spoken: S.R., between 21° S. and R. Limpopo, from Pafuri to below Muxecua, north-westwards almost to 30° E., eastwards to 32° 30′ E.

DSB names two subdivisions: MAKWAKWE and KHAMBANA.

TSWA (ʃi-)
Where spoken: P.E.A., on the coast just north of R. Save to south of Inhambane (excluding a strip between Porta de Barra Falsa and Jangamo); in the north the area extends westwards as far as the Save–Lundi confluence.

DSB distinguishes two dialects: DZIBI and DZONGA.

CHOPI GROUP

Where spoken: P.E.A.

DSB	MG3		*Other names*
CHOPI	COPI (ʃi-)	S.61/*	Tschopi, Lenge
LENGE			
TONGA	TONGA (gi-)	S.62/*	Shengwe

This Group is called 'Inhambane' (a geographical name) by DSB.

CHOPI (ʃi-)

Where spoken: On the coast east of the mouth of R. Limpopo as far as Jangamo, northwards between the Limpopo and 34° 30′ E., as far as 22° 30′ S.

Used in religious instruction.

LENGE is an archaic form, now disappearing, but still known to older women.[1]

TONGA (gi-)

Where spoken: On the coast, in a strip 10–20 miles wide between Porta de Barra Falsa and Jangamo.

There are no distinct dialectal forms (DSB).

[1] Earthy, 'A Story in KiLenge' (*Africa*, 1931).

UMBUNDU GROUP[1]

Where spoken: A.

MG3		Other names
MBUNDU (u-)	R.11/*	M'Bundo, Quimbundo, Kimbunda, Nano, Mbali, Mbari
NDOMBE	R.12/0	
NYANEKA (lu-)	R.13/0	
		HUMBE (DSB)
		MWILA (DSB), Muila, Huila

UMBUNDU, spoken by the ovi-MBUNDU

Where spoken: In the Benguela coastlands, eastwards to the upper Cuanza and Kweli rivers, from R. Cuvo in the north, southwards for over 200 miles.

Number: 1,331,087 (1940 Census).

NDOMBE

Where spoken: On the coast from near Benguela in the north to the lower Cunene river in the south, and eastwards to the middle Cunene.

There appears to be no linguistic information.

NYANEKA (lu-)

Where spoken: On the upper Cubango river, 14° 20′–15° 40′ S., westwards to R. Cunene, eastwards to 18° 40′ E.

DSB refers to 'the Nyaneka group' of many little-known dialects, of which he names HUMBE and MWILA.

'In general structure ... Umbundu shows remarkable similarity in grammar and vocabulary to Luena, Luchazi and other languages of the Ganguella group' (C. M. N. White).[2] Childs,[3] however, suggests that this is due to the dominating influence of UMBUNDU spoken in Viye, where the NYANGELA influence is strong, and to the relatively large number of missions in the Viye area.

See note on NGANGELA on pp. 67–68.

[1] The name is here used with prefix (u-) in order to distinguish it from ki-MBUNDU (see p. 63).
[2] In McCulloch, *The Ovimbundu* (Eth. Survey, 1952).
[3] *Umbundu Kinship and Character*.

KUANYAMA GROUP

Where spoken: A., S.W.A.

MG3		*Other names*
KUANYAMA (oci-)	R.21/*	Cuanhama, Kwanyama, Oshikuanjama, Osikuanjama, Ovambo, Humba
NDONGA (oci-)	R.22/*	Ambo, Oshindonga, Osindonga

KUANYAMA (oci-)

Where spoken: A., S.W.A., mainly west of the middle Cuango river, westwards to R. Cunene, 16°–17° 30′ E.

Used to a certain extent by missions in S.W.A.

NDONGA (oci-)

Where spoken: S.W.A., in a belt about 100 miles wide, 13° 30′–21° 20′ E.

HERERO SINGLE UNIT

Where spoken: S.W.A.

	MG3	Other names
HERERO	R.31:	
⎧ HERERO	R.31a/*	Otjiherero, Otyiherero
⎨ MBANDIERU	R.31b/o	
⎩ CIMBA	R.31c/o	Himba, Tjimba, Simba

HERERO

Where spoken: In two large enclaves (*a*) a belt only a few miles from the coast, 18° 30′–22° 30′ S.; (*b*) in the Epukiro and Waterberg Reserves, Okombahe, Otjihorongo and Ngamiland, in the Zesfontein Reserve in the Kaokoveld, and in urban areas (Windhoek, Okahandja, Omaruru, &c.).

Dialects:

HERERO, in the southern part of area (*a*) and most of area (*b*).
MBANDIERU, in the extreme east of area (*b*).
CIMBA, in the north-western part of area (*a*), extending into Angola.

YEI SINGLE UNIT

Where spoken: B.P., throughout Ngamiland.

	MG3	Other names
YEI (ci-)	R.41/*	Yeei, Yeye, Yeyi, Koba

INDEX

Abo, 10, 11
Achawa, 134
Adjumba, 23
Adouma, 24
Adsawa, Adsoa, 134
Aduma, 24
Adyumba, 23
Akpwakum, 22
Akwa, 36
[Alị, 34]
Alombooki, 46, 47
Amarani, 127
Amba, 89, 91, 92
Ambali, 29
Ambaquista, 63
Ambo[1], 80, 82
Ambo[2], 139
Amboim, 64
Ambuella, Ambwela, 67
Amu, 126, 127
Angba, Aŋba, 43, 45
'Apagibeti', 43, 45
Apindji, 25
Arusha, 117
Asu, Athu, Aṭhu, 122
Aushi, 80, 81
Avək, 16, 17
Ayawa, Ayao, 134
Azɔm, 21, 22

Baagəto, 19, 20
Baakpe, Baakpe, 6
Baali[1] (Ngala Gr.), 37, 39
Baali[2] (Bali Gr.), 88, 92
Baati, 43, 45
'Baato ba Loi, 40
Babeda, Babera, Babila, Babira, 89
Babogoro, 86
Baboŋg, Babong, 3, 4
'Baca, 152, 153
Bacenga, 14, 15
Badjia, 16
Badjue, 19
Bafaw, 3
Bafia, 13, 14
Bafɔ, 3, 4
Bafök, Bafuk, 16
Bafwagada, 101, 102
Bafwakayi, 101, 102
Bafwandaka, 88
Bagandou, 33
Bagbele, 87
Baidumba, 88, 90
Bajue, 19, 20
Bajuni, 126, 127
Bakaka, 3
Bakem, 10
Bakisi, 93

Bakja, 16, 17
Bakogo, 8, 10, 11
Bakoko, N., 6, 8, 10, 11, 16, 18
Bakoko, S., 6, 8, 10
Bakolle, 6
Bakosi, Bakossi, 3
Bakota[1], 28
Bakota[2], Bakǫta, 33
Bakum, 22
Bakųndų, Bakundu, 1
'Bakundumu, 88
Bakutu, 48, 50
Bakwele, 19
Bakwiri, 6
Bali[1] (Teke-Yans Gr.), 29, 30
Bali[2] (Bwa), 43
Bali[3], Balị, 88, 92
Balika, 101, 102
Balobo, 37
Balǫbo, 37
Baloi, 37, 40
Balom, 13
Balondo, Balondo, 3, 4
Baloŋ, Balong, 3, 6, 8, 10, 11
Balundu, 1
Balung, 3
Baluombila, 46, 47
Bambeiro, 63
Bambo, 82
Bamboko, Bambuku, 6
'Bambole', 46, 47
Bambuti, 89
Bambutuku, 101
[Bamileke, 4]
Bamitaba, 34
Bamvele, 16
Banaka, 9
Bandzabi, 27
Bane, 16
Banęka, 3, 4
Banen, Banen, Banend, 10, 11–12
Bangala, 38, 41
Bangandou, 33
Bangantu, N., 19, 20
'Bangba', 86
'Bangbinda, 87
Bangele, 37
'Bangelima', 43, 45
Bangi, 37
Bango, 43
Bangǫbangǫ, 72, 92
Bangomo, 24
Bangubangu, 72, 73, 92, 93
Bankǫn, Bankon, Baŋkǫn, 10, 11
Bankutu, 52
Banɔɔ, Banoho, 9
Banza, 37, 39
Baonga, 38, 42

Bape, 13
Bapǫkǫ, 9
'Bara' Swahili, 129
Bareko, 3, 4
Barombi, 10–11
Baryɛ, 1, 2
[Barumbi, 90]
Basa, 10–12
Basoa-Basoko, 38, 42, 46
Basɔkɔ, 38
Basosi, 3
Bassa, 10
Batanga[1], Bataŋga (Lundu Gr.), 1, 2
Batanga[2] (Bube Gr.), 9
Batị[1] Bati ('Sanaga' Gr.), 14, 15
Batị[2] (Baati), 43
Batwa, 107
Bavek, 16
Bëbëlë, 16, 17
Beeke, 101, 102
Beembe[1] (Kongo Gr.), 57, 60
Beembe[2] (Lega and Shi-Hunde Groups), 92, 93, 97, 98
Beena Tubeya, 68
Beke, 89, 90
Bekeni, 88
Bekke, 13
Bekpa, 13
Bɛkwịl, 19, 20
Bemba, Bemba, 80–82
Bembe[1], Bɛmbe (Ngala Gr.), 37, 39
Bembe[2] (Beembe[1]), 57
Bembe[3], Bɛmbɛ (Beembe[2]), 92, 97, 98
Bemili, 88
Bena, 131
Bënë, 16, 18
Bende, 118
Benga, 9
Benge, 43, 45
Beo, 43
Bethen, 19, 21, 22
Betsiŋga, Betzinga, 14, 15
Biakumbo, 2
Bịdjụkị, 19, 20, 21
Biisa, 80, 81
Bikum, 21
Bila[1], Bịla, 89
Bila, Bila[2], 155, 156
Bile, 80
Bili, 89, 90
Bịma, 1, 2
Bimbia, 6
Bindja, 43
Bindji, 72
Binja[1] (Binza), 43

INDEX

Binja², 92, 93
Binji, 72–73
Binza, 43, 44
Bira, 89–91
[Biri, 86]
Biriwa, 144, 146, 148, 150
Bisa, 80
Bisiwo, 19
Bito¹ (Nande Gr.), 95
Bito² (Huma), 107
Bǫa, 43
Bǫbangi, Bobangi, 37, 40
Bǫbɛa, Bobea, Bobe, 6
Bobili(s), 16
Boca, 'Boca, 144
Bǫdjman, Bodiman, 6, 7
Bodjinga, 39
Bodo, Bɔdɔ, 86, 87
Bodzanga, 33
Bogɔngɔ, Bǫgɔngǫ, 34, 35
Bogulu, 45
Boguru, 86, 87
Boko, 37, 39
Bokula, 39
Bǫlja, Bolia, 37, 39, 40, 48, 50
Bolo, 63, 64
Bologi, Bǫlǫkj, Boloki, 37, 38, 39, 41, 42
Boloki of Ruki, 48, 50
Bolondo, 37, 40
Bo-lɔngɔ, 48
Boma¹, 29, 31
Boma² (Boõ), 29
Boman, 20
Bombi, 101
Bombo, 19
Bǫmbǫkǫ, Bomboko, 6
Bomboli, Bombongo, 34, 35, 37
Bomvana, 152, 153
Bǫmwali, 19, 21
Bonde, Bondei, 122
Bondo, 64
'Bondokoyi, 40
Bɔnɛk, 10, 12
Bongili¹ (Bogɔngɔ), 34
Bǫngjlj, Bongili², Bongiri, 34, 35
Bonkembe, 39
Bɔnkɛŋ, Bɔŋkɛŋ, Bonkeng, Bonken Pendia, 3, 4, 6, 8, 10, 11
Boõ, 29, 30
Boro, 43, 45
Bɔswa, 7
Bota, 6
Botunga, 50
Boulou, 16
Boumboum, 19
Boyela, 52
Bubɛ, Bube, Bubi, 9
Bubj, 24
Budja, 42, 43
Budu, 101–2
Budya, 'Budya, 143

Buela, 43
Buende, 57
Buganza, S., 104
Bugombe, 88, 90
Bųja, 38, 39, 42, 43, 44
Bujwe, 92
Bukala, 48, 49
Bukongo, 34
Bukur, Bukuru, 86
Bukusu, 110
Bulebule, 89
Bųlų, Bulu¹, 16, 17, 18
Bulu², 24
Buluki, 37
Buma, 29
Bumbira, 104
Bumbuko, 6
Bunda, 58, 62
Bundum, 14
Bungiri, 34
Bungu, 119
Bunja, 66
Bunji, 'Bunji, 144
Buru, 43
Bushɔɔŋ, Bushongo, 54
Buulj, 48, 49
Buya, 110
Buyi, 97, 98
Buyu, 92
Bvanuma, 101
Bvumba, 144
Bwa, 43, 44–45
Bwari, 98
Bweende, Bwende, 57, 60
Bwɛla, 43, 44
Bwila, Bwile, Bwilɛ, 80, 81
Bwili, 7
Bwisi, Bwisi, 105, 108

Caga, 117
Cewa, 139, 140
Chaga, Chagga, 117
Chasu, 122
Cheva, Chewa, Cheŵa, 139
Chiga, 105
Chikunda, 141
Chiluba (Sanga), 72
Chinimakonde, 134
Chinyanja, 139
Chishona, Chiswina, 143
Chokwe, 67–69
Chonyi, 126
Chopi, 157
Chuabo, 135
Chuana, 148
Chuka, 115, 125
Chwabo, 135
Cifundi, 126, 127
Ciga, 105
Ciina Mukundi, 83
Cikunda, 141
Cikuya, 29

Cikwakwa, 143
Cilowe, 135
Cimba, 160
Cjnga, 14, 15
Cioko, Ciokwe, 67
Cipeta, 139
Coana, 148
Cokwe, 67
Congo (Kongo), 56
Conyi, 126, 129
Copi, 157
Cuabo, Cuambo, 135
Cuana, 148
Cuanhama, 159

Daḅida, Dabida, 125
Dadiri, 110
Dande, 144
Dembo, 64
Dɛngɛsɛ, 54
Dhaiso, 115, 116
Dĭ, 29, 31
Dianga, 43, 44
Dibeng, 10
Djḅųm, 10, 11
Digo, 125, 126, 129
Dika, 59
Diŋ, 29, 31
Dirico, Diriko, Diriku, 66
Djanti, 13
Djao, 134
Djem, 19
Djembe, 54
Djja, 29, 31, 49, 51
Djikini, 29
Djok, 67
Djonga, 155
Doe, 123
Dǫgwa, 149, 151
Dohe, 123
'Doko, Dɔkɔ, 43, 44
Domba, 'Domba, 144
Dongo, 63, 65
Doombi, 90
Doondo, 57, 60
Douala, 6
Douma, 24
Doumbou, 28
Dschagga, 117
Dschogni, 126
Duala, Dųala, 6–8
Dųma, Duma¹, 24, 27
'Duma, Duma², 143, 145
Duruma, 126, 127
Dyųmba, 23
Dzalamo, 123
Dzibi, 155, 156
Dzihana, 126
Dzimu, 19
Dzindza, 104, 106
Dziŋ, Dzing, 29, 31
Dzonga, 155, 156

INDEX

Edangabo, 104
Ediya, 9
Eki, 16, 17, 18
Ekonda, 48, 50
Ekumbe, 1, 2
Eleko, 38
Ɛlembɛ, 52
Eling, 10
Elong, 3
Embu, Ɛmbọ, 115
Embuja, 43
Ɛna, 103
Enenga, 23
Enya, 103
Epigi, 28
Esel, 20
Eso, 46
Etọn, 16
Evuzok, 16
Ewodi, 6
Ewọndọ, Ewondo, 16, 17

Fa', Fak, 13
'Fanakalo, Fanekalo', 152, 154
Faŋ, Fan̄, Fañwe, Fang, 18
Fernandian, 9
Fingo, 152
'Fiot, Fiote', 57, 58, 60, 62
Fipa, 76, 80, 82
Fọma, 46, 47, 48, 50
Fuliiru, 97
Fulilwa, 137
Fuliro, 97, 99, 100
Fulirwa, 137, 138
Fuluka, 52
Fuma, 46, 47, 48, 50
Fumu, 29, 30
Fuŋ, 10, 12
Fungwe, 137, 138
Furiiro, 97

Gaangala, 57, 60
Gaika, 152, 153
Galoa, Galwa, 23
Gananwa, 148
Ganda, 105, 108-9
Ganga, 54
'Ganguella', 67
Ganza, 104, 107
Garaganza, 119
Garwe, 144
'Gɛvamenti' Swahili, 129
Gaya, 109
Gbati, 86
[Gbaya, 22, 34]
Gbïgbïl, 16, 17
[Gbofi, 34]
Gbote, 86
Gcaleka, 152, 153
Gciriku, 66
Gẹkọyọ, 115

Gendja, 43
Gendza-Baali, 43
Gengele, 92, 93
Genia, 103
Genja, 43
Genya, 92, 94, 103
Gezon, 43
Gikuyu (Kikuyu), 115, 128
Gimbunda, 67
Ginga, 63
Girango, 113, 114
Giriama, Giryama, 126, 129
Gishu, Gisu, 110
Goba[1] (Mbukushu), 66
Goba[2], 143, 145
Gobera, 143, 145
Gogo, 121
Goma 98
Gongo, 54
Gova, 143
Goya, 66
Govara, 143
Guha, 92
Gungu, 105
Guru, 86
Gusii, Gusii, Gusii, 113
Guta, 144
Guzii, 113
Gwamba, Gwapa, 135
Gwe[1], 111, 112
Gwe[2] (Sukuma), 119
Gweno, 117, 122
Gwere, 105, 109

Ha, 100
Haavu, 97
Hadimu, 126, 127
Hai, 117
Haiao, 134
Haka, 63
Hamba[1] (Tetela Gr.), 52
Hamba[2] (Amba), 89
Hamba[3] (Inter-Lacustrine Gr.), 104
Hambo, 95, 96
Hanga, 111, 112
Hangaza, 100
Hangiro, 104
Haraba, Harava, 143
Havu, 97
Haya, 104, 106
Hehe, 131-2
Hema, 105, 107
Hemba, Hemba, 72, 74
Henga, 137
Hera, 104
Here, 144
Herero, 160
Heso, 46
Hewa, Hewe, 137, 138
Hiao, 134
Hima, 105, 107, 108

Himba, 160
'Hindi' Swahili, 129
Hinzua, 126
Hira, 95
Hlanganu, 155, 156
Hlengwe, 155, 156
Hlubi, 152, 153
Hoko, 101
Hokohoko, 89, 90
Holoholo, 92, 93, 94
Holo, Holu, 58, 61, 63, 65
Homa, 86, 87
Homba, 95
Hombo, 49
Horohoro, Hororo, 105, 108
Hɔrɔhɔrɔ, 92
Huana, 57
Huila, 158
Huku, 101
Humba, 159
Humbe[1] (Lilima), 144
Humbe[2], 158
Humu, 89, 91
Hunde[1] (Kobi), 95
Hunde[2], 97, 98
Hungana, Huŋanna, Hungaan, 57, 61, 65
Hungo, Hungu, 58, 59, 60, 61, 62, 65
Hungwe, 144
Hurutshe, Hurutsi, 148, 150
Hutu, 104, 106-7
Hwindja, 97, 98
Hyanzi, Hyanzi, 89, 91

Idakho, Idaxo, 111, 112
Idzing, 29
Ifumu, 29
'Ikeleve' Kongo, 62
Ikenga, 35
Ikizu, 113, 114
Ikoma, 113
Ikuhani, Ikwahane, 83, 85
Ila, 83-84
Ileo, 54
Ima, 1
Imilangu, 70
Imoma, 48, 50
Inamwanga, 77
Ingondi, 34
Inja, 48, 50
Iramba, 120
Irangi, 120
Iru, 105
Isenyi, 113, 114
Isongo, 33
Isu, Isubu, Isuwu, 6, 7
Isukha, Isuxa, 111, 112
Itokho, 111
Itumba, 123
Itundu, 10
Iwa, 77, 78, 79

INDEX

Jamba-Makutu, 37
Jaunde, 16
Jena, 143, 145
Jibana, 126, 129
Jindwi, 144
Jinga, 63
Jinja, 104
Jita, 104, 105
Jonga, 155, 156
Jɔnga, 52, 53

Kaa, 3, 4
Kaalɔŋ, 13
Kaamba, 57, 60
Kaanu, 92, 93
Kabwari, 97, 98
Kaffer, Kaffir, 152
Kagulu, Kaguru, 121, 124
Kahe, 117
Kahonde, 72
Kaiku, 89
Kaka¹, 21, 22
Kaka² of Sala, 19, 20
Kaka³, 22
Kakamega, 111
Kakelelwa, 111, 112
Kakɔ, 22
Kakumega, 111
Kala, 48
Kalanga¹ (Lega Gr.), 92, 94
Kalanga², Kalaŋa, Kalaŋga, Kalaka, Kalana, 144, 145–6
Kalebwe, 72
Kalo, 52
Kamanga, 137
Kamba, 115, 116
Kambe, 126, 129
Kambonsenga, 82
Kami, 123, 124
Kańandjoho, 28
Kandawire, 137, 138
Kande, 25
Kanga, 59
Kangama, 38, 42
Kango, 43, 45
Kaninkin, 68
Kanioka, Kanyoka, Kanyɔka, 72, 74
Kaonde, 72, 74, 80, 82
Kara, 104, 106
Karagwe, 105, 107
Karanga, Karaŋa, 143, 145
Kare, Kari, 86
Karombe, 144
Kauma, 126, 129
Kawanga, 111
Kawonde, 72
Keembo, 48, 50
Kela, Kɛla, 52, 53
Kɛlɛ, 24
Kele¹ (Ngala Gr.), 38, 41
Kɛlɛ, Kele², 46–47, 49, 50

Kenyi, 105, 109
Kerebe, Kerebe, Kerewe, 104, 105–6
Kete, 72
Kgaga, 148
Kgalagadi, 148
Kgatla, 148
Khalahadi, 148
Khambana, 155, 156
Khatla, 148, 150
Khayo, 111
Khutshwe, Khutswe, Khutswi, 149
Khutu, 123
Kibala, 64
Kichi, 133
Kiga¹, 104, 105, 107, 108
Kiga² (Tshiga), 104
Kikete, 72
Kikuyu, 115–16, 125
Kimambwe, 76
Kimawanda, 134
Kimbu, 119
Kimbunda¹, 67
Kimbunda² (Umbundu), 158
Kimbundu, 59, 62, 63–64
Kimbundu of Nambuangongo, 59, 62, 63, 64
Kimbuti, 89
Kinga, 79
Kiŋga, 79, 131
Kingwana, 81, 126, 128
[Kipsigis, 128]
Kira, 95, 96
Kiroba, 113, 114
Kisa, 111, 112
Kisi, Kisii¹, 131, 132
Kisii² (Gusii), 113
Kissama, 63, 64
Kisu, 110
'Kitchen Kaffir', 152, 154
Kitosh, 110
Kiya, 119
Koba, 70
Kobi, 95, 96
Koena, 148
Kogoro, 86, 87
Koko, 10
Kɔlɛ, 6, 7
Kololo, 69, 70, 71, 151
Kɔmbɛ, 9
Kombe, 14
Komo, Kɔmɔ, 89, 92
Kɔnabɛm, Kɔnabɛmb, Kɔnabembe, 19, 20
Konde¹ (Ngonde), 79
Konde², 155
Kondjo, 95
Kondoa, 123
Kongo¹ (Wɔngo), 55
Kongo², 56–62
Kongola, 52

Kongola-Meno, 52
Koŋwala, 35
Koni, 148, 150
Konjo, 95
Kɔnɔngo, 119
Kɔnzo, Konzo, 95, 96, 108
Kooki, 104, 106
Koongo, 56, 57, 58, 59, 60, 61
Kɔɔsë, Kɔɔsɔ, 3, 5
Korekore, 143, 145
Kɔrja, 113
Kosova, 113
Kɔta¹, Kota, 24
Kɔta² (Ngando Gr.), 33
Koukouya, 29
Kɔyɔ, 36
Kozime¹ (Njëm), 19
Kozime², 20
Kpa, 13
Kpabili, 21
Kpala, 34
Kpe, 6
Kuanyama, 159
Kuba, 36
Kuba, 49, 54–55, 72, 73
Kukuya, Kukẅa, 29, 30
Kukwe, 79
Kuma, 117
Kumbule, 95, 96
Kumu, 89
Kunda¹ (Ngombe Gr.), 43, 44
Kunda² (Nsenga Gr.), 141
Kundu, 1
Kunyi, 57, 60
Kurja, Kuria, Kurya, 113
Kusu, Kusu, 52
Kutswe, 149
Kutu¹ (Yɛla), 52
Kutu², 123, 124
Kuumu, 89, 90, 92
Kuundji, 59
Kuya, 28
Kwachikwakwa, 143
Kwakum, 22
Kwala, 36
Kwandi, 70, 71
Kwangali, Kwangari, 66
Kwangwa, 70, 71
Kwanyama, 159
Kwaya, 104, 105
Kwazvimba, Kwazwimba, 143
Kwe, 29, 30
Kwena, 148, 150
Kwenyi, 123
Kwese, Kwɛsɛ, 57, 61
Kxalaxarj, 148, 150
Kxatla, Kxhatla, 148, 150
Kxaxa, 148, 150

Laadi, 57
Laali, 29, 30
Ladi, 57

INDEX

Lala¹ (Bemba Gr.), 80, 81, 82
Lala² (Nguni Gr.), 152
Lali, 29, 30
Lalja, Lalia, 48, 50
Lamba, 80, 82
Lambia, Lambya, Lambwa, 77, 78, 137, 138
Lamu, 126
Langa, 52, 53
Lange, 72, 73
Langi, Langi, 120
Lari, 57, 60
Leedji, 89, 90
Leega, 92, 93
Lega¹ (Bira Gr.), 89, 91
Lega², Lɛga, 92–94, 96, 98
Lega³ (Nande Gr.), 95
Lega⁴ (Bafwagada), 101
Lękǫ, Lɛku, 38, 42
Lele, Lɛlɛ, 54, 55
Lemande, 10
Lemba, 52
Lembue, 80, 81
Lenge, 157
Lengola, Lɛngɔla, 89, 90, 92, 94, 103
Lengue, 64
Lenje, 83
Lepɔk, 16, 17
Lera, 104, 107
'Leta' Kongo, 62
Lete, 148, 150
Lewi, 111
Leya, 83, 84
Libenge, 43
Libinja, Libinza, 37, 39
Libolo, 63
Libwali, 43
Likila, 37, 39
Liko, 88
Likolo, 46, 47
Likouala, Likwala, 36
Lileko, 47
Lilima, 144, 145
Limba, 6
Limi, 120
Lindja, 97, 98
Lingala, 38, 41, 42
Lingbe, 86
Lingi, 43
Linyeli, Linzeli, 34
Lipanja, 37, 39
Lissongo, 33
Liutwa, 46, 47
Llǫgǫle, 113
Loango, 57
Lobala, 34, 35
Lobedu, 149
Lobo, 37, 39
Logananga, 10
Logooli, 113
Lɔj, Loi, 37, 39–40

Lokele, 46, 47
Lokundu, 1
Lolo¹ (Nkųndǫ), 48
Lolo² (Lomwe), 135
'Lololo', 152, 154
Lombi, 10, 11
Lombǫ, 46
Lombooki, 46, 47
Lomongo, 48
Lomotua, Lomotwa, Lɔmɔtwa, 80, 81
Lomwe, 135, 142
Lɔŋ, 3, 5
Lɔŋgo, 48, 50
Longe-Longe, 97, 98
Lonkundu, 48
Lɔsɛngɔ, Lɔsɛŋgɔ, 38, 40, 42
Louyi, 70
Lovale, 67
Lovedu, 149
Lozi, 69, 70, 71, 149, 151
Luangu, 57, 60
Luano¹ (Luyana), 70
Luano², 80, 82
Luba, Luba, 54, 72–74
Lubala, 67
Lubedu, 149, 151
Lucazi, Luchazi, 67, 68
Lue, 1
Luena, 67
Luganda, 105
Luguru, 123
Luhya, 111–12
Lui, Luiana, 70
Luimbe, Luimbi, 67, 68
Luizi, 70
Lujazi, 67
Lukolwe, 75
Luku, 54
Lulua, 72, 73
Luluhya, Luluyia, 111
Lumbo, 62
Lumbu, 26
Luna, 72, 73
Lunda, 67, 69
Lunda, N., 67
Lundu, 1–2
Lundwe, 83, 84
Lungu, 76
Lungulu, 79
Luntu, 72, 73
Lunyankole, 105
[Luo, 109, 128]
Lupanga, 129
Lusengo, 38
Lushange, 75
Luula, 56, 59, 62
Luunda, 67
Luuwa, 58, 61
Luya, 72
Luvale, 67
Luyana, Luyi, 70–71, 84, 151

Luyia, 111
Luwunda, 67
Lwalu, 72, 73
Lwena, 67, 68–69
Lwimbi, 67
Lwindja, 97

[Maasai, 116, 128]
Mabaale, 37, 39
[Mabadi, 86]
Mabale, 37
Mabea, Mabi, 19
Mabiha, 134
Mabiti, 88
Macamba, 64
Macame, Machame, Madschame, 117
Maganja, 139
Mahongwe, 24
Mäkaa, Makaa, Maka, 18, 19–21, 22
Makamba, 64
Makanga, 139
Make, 16, 18
Makoa, Makoane, 135
Makoda, 101, 102
Makoma, 70, 71
Makonde, 134
Makua, Makwa, 135
Makwakwe, 155, 156
Mala, 83, 84
Malamba, 101, 102
Malawi, 135
Maliko, 88
Malila, 77
Malimba, 6
Mambukush, 66
Mambwe, 76, 80, 81
Mampoko, 37
Mampukush, 66
Manda, 136
Mandi, 10, 12
Manehas, 3
Mangala, 38, 41
Mananja, Mang'anja, Mangandja, 139, 140, 141
Manganji, 37
Mangbele, 86, 87
[Mangbetu, 86, 87, 88]
Mangisa, Mangisa, 14
Mangwato, 148
Manyika, 144, 145
Maraci, 111, 112
Maragoli, 113
Marama, 111, 112
Marangu, 117
Marave, Maravi, 135, 139, 140, 141
Mari, 143
Masaba, 110
Masanze, 92, 94
Masemola, Masemula, 148, 150

INDEX

Mashami, 117
Mashasha, 75
Mashi, 70, 71
Maswaka, 80
Mate, 95
Matengo, 132, 136, 139, 140
Matta, 101, 102
Matųmbį, Matumbi, 131, 132, 133
Mavia, Maviha, Mawia, Maŵiha, 134
Mawisi, 105
Mayeka, 86
[Mayogo, 87]
Mazaro, 139, 140
Mbaama, 28
Mbaamba, 56, 59
Mbagani, 73
Mbai, 149
Mbaka, 63, 64
Mbala¹ (Bụshɔɔŋ), 54
Mbala² (Kongo Gr.), 57, 60
Mbala³ (Kongo Gr.), 58, 61, 65
Mbala⁴ (Luba Gr.), 72, 73
Mbalazi, 126, 127
Mbale, 54
Mbali, 158
Mbam, 14
Mbamba¹ (Mbaama), 28
Mbamba², 63, 64
Mbande, 68
Mbandieru, 160
Mbangala, 58, 62, 63, 64, 65, 67, 69
Mbaŋg, 10, 11
Mbaŋwɛ, 24
Mbari, 158
Mbata, 56, 59
Mbatį, 33, 34
Mbati-Ngombe, 44
Mbayi, 149
Mbede, 28
Mbeeko, 57, 59
Mbɛnɛ, 10, 11
Mbengi, 54
Mbensa, Mbinsa, 57
Mbɛsa, Mbesa, 38, 42, 46
Mbętę, 28
Mbimu, 19, 20
Mbinga, 37, 39
Mbinsa, 57, 60
Mbire, 143
Mbo¹, Mbɔ, 3-5
Mbo² (Nyali Gr.), 101, 102
Mbo³ (Nyanja), 139, 140
Mbogedu, 66
Mboka, 57, 60
Mboko, 6
Mbọkọ, 36
Mbɔlɛ, Mbole, 48, 50, 103
Mboma, 56, 59
Mbọmọtaba, 34, 35, 41

Mbɔŋ, 13
Mbɔŋge, Mbɔŋgɛ, 1, 2
Mbooso, 46, 47
Mbosį, Mboshi, 36
Mbowe, 70
Mbųdza, 38, 41
Mbugwe, 120
Mbuiyi, 64
Mbukuhu, Mbukushu, 66
Mbuli, 52, 53
[Mbum, 22]
Mbumbum, 19
Mbunda¹ (Mbuun), 29
Mbunda² (Chokwe-Lunda Gr.), 67, 69
Mbunda³ (Luyana Gr.), 70
Mbundjo, 34
M'Bundo, 158
Mbundu, ki-, 63
Mbundu, u-, 158
Mbundza, 66
Mbunga, 133
Mbunu, 29
Mbuun, 29, 31
Mbuunda (Mbunda²), 67
Mbuti, 89
Mbwela, Mbwera, 67, 68, 69, 72, 74, 75
Mɛdjįmɛ, Mɛdjįmę, 19, 20
Medo, 135
Medzime, 19
Megi, 121
Meŋgaŋ, 16, 17
Mɛrọ, Meru, 115
Metoko, 92
Mfengu, 152, 154
Mfinu, 29, 31
Mfumu, 29
Mfununga, 29
Mhari, 143, 145
Mihavane, Mihavani, Mihawani (Ngulu²), 135
Mindųųmọ, 28
Minungo, 58
Mishulundu, 70, 71
Mitsogo, 25
Mituku, Mįtųkų, 89, 90, 92, 94, 103
Moci, 117
Mokpę, Mokpe, 6
Mombe, 79
Mombesa, 38
[Mondjombo, 34, 35]
Mongo¹ (Mųngọ), 6
Mongo² (Bụshɔɔŋ), 54
Mongo³, Mongo, Mɔŋgɔ, 47, 48-51, 53
Moshi, 117
Mpaangu, 56, 59
Mpako, 56
Mpama, 48, 49
Mpasu, 72, 73

Mpɛsa, 38, 41
Mpese, 56, 59
Mpjɛmɔ, 19, 20-21
Mpɔ̃mpɔ̃, Mpompo, 19, 20
Mpondo, 151, 152
Mpondomisi, Mpondomse, 152, 153
Mpoŋgo, 48, 50
Mpongoué, Mpɔŋgwę, 23
Mpoto, 136
Mpũ, Mpũmpũ, 29
Mpukushu, 66, 70, 71
Mrima, 126, 127
Mtaŋata, 126, 127
Muamenam, 3
Muenyi, 70
Muila, 158
Mųlįmba, 6, 8
Mumbala (Mbala²), 57
Mųngọ, Mųŋgọ, 6, 7
Mussende, 64
Musserongo, 56
Mvang, 16, 18
Mvang Makona, 18
Mvele, 10
Mvëlë, 16, 17
Mvita, 126, 127
Mvumbo, 19
Mwahɛt, 3, 5
Mwali, 128
Mwamba, 79
Mwanga, 77, 80, 82
Mwani, 104
Mwela, 134
Mwenyi, 70, 71
Mwera, 134
Mwerį, 119
Mwila, 158
Myɛnɛ, Myene, 23

Naka, 9
Nambzya, 144, 146
Namwanga, 77
Namwezi, 119
Nande, Nandi, 95-96
[Nandi, 109, 112, 128]
Nano, 158
'Napagibetini', 43, 45
'Napagisene', 43, 45
'Napagitene', 43, 45
Nari, 150
Nata, 113, 114
Nbundo, N'Bundo, 63
Ncqika, 152
Ndaaka, 101, 102
Ndaanda, 34
Ndali¹ (Nyiha-Safwa Gr.), 77, 78
Ndali² (Gusii Gr.), 113, 114
Ndamba, 130
Ndande, Ndandi, 95
Ndara, 104, 107
Ndau, 144, 145

INDEX

Nde'bele, Ndebele, 152, 153
Ndɛmbɔ, Ndembu, 67, 69
Ndengereko, 133
Ndengese, Ndɛngɛsɛ, 54
Ndibu, 56, 59
Ndingi, Ndinzi, 57, 60
Ndjabi, 27
Ndjeli, Ndjɛli, 34
Ndjëm, 19
Ndjembe, 54
Ndjevi, 27
Ndjinini, 29
Ndlambe, 152, 153
Ndogbang, 10
Ndogbanol, 10
Ndogo, 104
Ndokama, 10
Ndokbele, 10
Ndokbiakat, 10
Ndokpenda, 10
Ndoktuna, 10
Ndolo, 37
Ndombe, 158
Ndonde, 134
Ndonga, 159
Ndoongo, 63
Ndoobo, 37, 39
Ndoolo, 37, 40
Ndorwa, 104, 107
Nduga, 104, 107
Ndumu, 28
Ndundulu, 70, 71
Ndzikou, Ndzindzihu, 29
Ndzundza, 149, 151, 152, 154
Nɛnũ, 3, 5
Ngage, 64
Ngala, 37–42
Ngande, 54
Ngandǫ¹, Ngando, 33
Ngandǫ², Ŋgando (Mongo-Nkundo Gr.), 48, 50
Ngangela, Ngangwela, 67
Ngangoulou, Ngangulu, 29
Ngarɛ, 36
Ngayaba, Ŋgayaba, 13
Ngazidja, Ngazija, 126, 128
[Ngbaka Mabo, 34]
Ngbee, 86, 87
Ngbinda, 86, 87
Ŋee, 29, 30
Ŋgele, 38, 42
Ngelima, 43
Ŋgɛn, 3
Ngengu, 64
Ŋhwele, Nghwele, 123
Ngịndo, Ngindo, 133
Ngingi, 57
Ngịrị, Ngiri, 37, 39
Ngoba, 143, 145
Ngole, 63
Ngolo, 1
Ngɔm, 24

Ngoma, 80, 81
Ngombe¹, Ngɔmbɛ, 43–45
Ngombe², Ngombia, 54
Ngonde, 79
Ngǫndị, Ŋgǫndị, 34
Ngongo¹ (Tetela Gr.), 52
Ngongo² (Kuba Gr.), 54
Ngoni¹, Tanganyika, 136, 153
Ngoni², N. Rhodesia, 140, 153
Ngoni³, Nyasaland, 152, 153
Ngoongo, 58, 61
Ngoreme, 113
Ngǫrǫ, Ŋgǫrǫ, 1
Ngɔrɔ, Ŋgɔrɔ, 14
Ngova, Ŋgoa, 143
Ngoy¹ (Kongo Gr.), 56, 59, 60
Ngoy² (Bweende), 57
Ngoyo, 57
Ngruimi, 113
Ngul, 32
Ngulu¹ (Zaramo Gr.), 123
Ngulu² (Makua Gr.), 135
Ngumba, 19
Ngumbi, 9
Ngundi, 34
Ngundji, 38, 41
Ngungulu, Ngungwel, Ngungwoni, 29, 30
Nguni, 136, 151, 152-4
Ngurimi, Nguruimi, 113, 114
Nguru¹ (Zaramo Gr.), 113
Nguru² (Makua Gr.), 135
Ŋgwaketsi, Ngwaketse, 148, 150
Ngwalungu, 155, 156
Ngwana, 81, 126, 128
Ŋwatu, Ŋwatụ, Ngwato, 148, 149
Niakiusa, 79
Nica, Nicat, Nika, 137
Nịlyamba, Nilyamba, Nịlamba, Nilamba, 120
Ninong, 3
Niramba, 120
Njabi, 26, 27
Njanja, 143
Njëm, 19, 20
Njikini, 29
Njinga, 63, 64
Njinịnị, 29
Njinju, 29, 30
Njuani, 126
Nkangala, 67, 68, 69
Nkanu, 57, 59
Ŋkembe, 48, 50
Nkole, 105
Ŋkole, 48
Nkɔmị, Nkomi, 23
Nkonde, 79
Nkore, 105, 108
Nkosi, 3, 5
Nkoya, 75
Nkucu, 52
Nkunda, 123

Nkụndǫ, Ŋkundo, Ŋkundo, 48, 49
Nkụtụ, Nkutu, Nkutshu, 52, 54
Nkwifiya, 123
Nobvu, 143
Nohwe, 143
Nɔɔ, Noho, Noko, 9
Npongué, 23
Nrebele, 149, 151, 152, 154
Nsenga, 82, 139, 141
Nsongo, 63, 64
Nsuundi, 56
Ntaandu, 56, 59
Nthali, 137, 138
Ntǫmba, Ntomba, 37, 39, 40, 48, 50
Ntsaayi, 29
Ntum, 16, 18
Nungo¹ (Kongo, &c., Groups), 58, 61, 67, 68
Nungo² (Shinji), 57
Nụnụ, 37, 40
Nwesi, 80, 81
Nyabungu, 97
Nyai, 144, 146
Nyakisasa, 104
Nyakusa, Nyakyusa, 79
Nyala, 105, 109, 111, 112
Nyali, 101
Nyambo, 105, 107
Nyamtam, Nyamtan, 10
Nyamuka, 144
Nyamwanga, 77
Nyamwesị, Nyamwesi, Nyamwezị, 119
Nyaneka, 158
Nyanga¹ (Kari Gr.), 86
Nyanga² (Lega and Nande Groups), 92, 93, 95, 96
Nyani, 28
Nyanja, 139–40, 153
Nyankore, 105
Nyanyembe, Nyanyembe, 119
Nyara, 105
Nyari, 101
Nyaruanda, Nyarwanda, 104
Nyasa¹ (Manda, Mpoto), 136
Nyasa² (Nyanja), 139
Nyaturu, 120
Nyatwe, 144
Nyɛkyǫsa, 79
Nyengo, 67, 69, 70, 71
Nyiha, Nyika¹, 77, 78
Nyika², 125, 126, 129
Nyika³ (Tumbuka), 137, 138
Nyikyusa, 79
Nyindu, 97, 98
Nyixa, 77
Nyokon, 10
Nyole, 111
Nyongwe, 143
Nyoole, 111
Nyɔ̃ɔ̃, 10, 12

INDEX

Nyore, 111
Nyoro, 105, 107, 109
Nyu'bi, Nyuɓi, Nyubi, 143, 145
Nyuli, 111
Nyungwe, 139, 140, 141
Nzɛbi, 27
Nzikini, 29
Nziku, Nzinzihu, 29
Nzombo, 56
Nzwani, 126, 128

Obamba, 28
Okande, 25
Ǫli, Oli, 7
Ɔli, 48
Ombo, Ɔmbo, 49, 51, 52, 53
Omvang, 16
Omyene, 23
Ondoumbo, 28
Orungu, 23
Oshikuanjama, Osikuanjama, 159
Oshindonga, Osindonga, 159
Otjiherero, Otyiherero, 160
Ovambo, 159

Pahouin, 18
Paj, Pai, 149, 151, 152, 154
Pakombe, 89
Pakum, 22
Pamue, 18
Pande, Pandɛ, Pande, 34-35
Panga¹ (Mongo-Nkundo Gr.), 48, 49
Panga² (Pianga), 54
Pangwa, 131, 132
Pangwe, 18
Pate, Patta, 126, 127
Patu, 57
Pedi, 148, 150-1, 154
Pemba, 126
Pende, Pɛndɛ, 57
Pendi, 57
Penin, Penyin, 10
Peri, 144
Pɛri, Pere, 89
Peta, 139, 140
Pfokomo, 125
Pfunde, 143
Phaku, 56
Phalaborwa, Phalaburwa, 148, 149, 150, 151
Phani, 147
Phatu, 57, 59
Phemba, 126, 127
Phoka, 137
Phuthi, 148, 149, 152, 153
Pianga, 54
Piindi, 57
'Piki', 152
Pili, 89
Pimbwe, 76
Pindi, Pinji, 57, 61

Podzo, 141, 142
Pogolo, Pogoro, 130, 131, 132
Poka, 137, 138
Pǫke, 46
Poko, 9
Pokomo, Pokomo, 125
Pǫl, 22
Pɔmɔ, 22
Pombo, 58
Ponda, 67
Ponek, 10
Pǫngǫ, Pɔŋgɔ, Pongo, 6, 7
Pongoué, 23
Poombo, 58, 61
Pǫto, Poto, 38, 41
Puku, 9
Pul, 22
Pylana, Pulana, 148, 150, 151, 154
Puna, 58, 62
Punu, 26

Quembo, 64
Quibala, 64
Quilengue, 64
Quimbundo, 158
Quissama, 63, 64
Qwabe, 152

Rabai, 126, 129
Ragoli, 113
Rebu, 37
Rega, 92
Rɛmi, 120
Rhinyirhinyi, 97, 98
Ribe, Rihe, 126, 127
Rimi, Rimi, 120
Roloŋ, Rolong, 148, 150
Rombi, 10
Rombo, 117
Ronga, 155
Rǫngǫ, 23
Rori, 131
Rotse, 70
Rouyi, 70
Rozi, Rozvi¹, 144, 145
Rozvi², Rozwi, 70
Ruanda, Rwanda, 104
Ruciga, 104
Rue, 141, 142
Rufiji, 123
Ruguru, 123, 124
Rujhi, 123
Rukiga, 104
Rundi, 100, 104, 106, 107
Rungu¹, 76, 80
Rungu² (Taabwa), 80
Rungwa, 76
Runyarwanda, 104
Rusha, 117
Ruundi, 67, 68
Rwanda, 100, 104, 106-7
Rwo, 117

Saamia, 111
Sabei, Bantu, 105
Safwa, 77, 78
Sagala, N.¹ (Kaguru), 121
Sagala² (Zaramo Gr.), 123, 124
Sagala³, Sagalla, 125
Sagara, 123
Sageju, 115
Sakani, Sakanyi, 48
Sakata, 29, 31, 49, 51
Salampasu, 72
Salya, 79
Sama, 63, 64
Samba, 65, 72, 74
Sambaa, Sambara, 122
Sambio, Sambiu, Sambyu, 66
Samia, Samya, 111
'Sanaga', 14-15
Sanga, 72, 74, 80, 82
Sango, Sangu¹, 131
Sangu² (Shira-Puna Gr.), 26
Santu, 62
Sanza, 95, 96
Sanzi¹ (Lega Gr.), 92, 93
Sanzi² (Shi-Hunde Gr.?), 98
Sassu, 62
'Saw', 37
Schambala, 122
Seba, 80, 82
Segeju, 115, 116
Sɛkiyani, 24
Selya, 79
Sena¹ (Maŋanja), 139
Sena² (Nsenga Gr.), 141
Senga¹ (Tumbuka Gr.), 137, 138
Senga² (Nsenga), 141
Sengeju, 115
Sɛngɛlɛ, 37, 40, 49
Seria, 79
'Serikali' Swahili, 129
Sese, 105, 109
'Settla, Settler' Swahili, 128
Sewa, Seɓa, 80
Sesuto, 148
Shaka, 117
Shake, 24
'Shamba' Swahili, 129
Shambaa, Shambala, 122, 123
Shanga, 144
Shangaan, 155
Shango, 26
Shangwe, Shaŋwe, 143, 145
Shanjo, 70, 71
Shankadi, 72
Sheetswa, 155
Shengwe (Tonga⁶), 157
Sheva, 139
Shi, 97-98
Shikalu, 75
Shila, 80, 81
Shinji, 57, 61, 65, 67, 68
Shioko, 67

INDEX

Shira¹ (Sira), 26
Shira² (Shaka Gr.), 117
Shishi, 80
Shoba, Shobya, 54
Shobyo, 104, 107
Shona, 143–6
Shongo, 54
Shu, 95, 96
Shubi, 100
Shukaali, 95, 96
Shukulumbwe, 83
Simaa, 70, 71
Simba, 160
Sįmbįtį, 113, 114
Singa, 105, 109
Sinja, 100
Sjora, 113, 114
Sira, 26
Siska, Sisya, 136
Siu, Siyu, 126, 127
So, 19
Sɔ, 46, 50
Sochile, 79
Sofala, 144
Soga, 105, 109
Sokile, Sokili, 79
Soko, Sɔkɔ, 46, 48, 50
Soli, 67, 68, 83
Solongo, 56, 59
Sondi, 56
Songe, Sɔŋge, Songi, 72, 73
Songo, 58, 63, 64, 67
Songola¹ (Mongo-Nkundo Gr.), 49, 51
Songola², Sɔngɔla (Lega Gr.), 92, 93
Sɔngɔmeno, 54, 55
Songoora, 95, 96
Songu, 58, 62, 63, 64, 67, 69
Sonjo, 113, 115
Soonde, 58, 61
Sooso, Soso, 56, 59
Sosso, 58
Sotho, Sɔthɔ, 71, 146, 148–51, 153, 154
Soubiya, 85
Sụ, 6, 7
Suaheli, 126
Subia, Subiya, 83, 84, 85
Subu, 6
Subya, 85
Suku, 58, 65, 67, 68
Sukulumbwe, 83
Sukuma, Sụkụma, 119
Sumbwa, 119
Sungu, 52
Suthu, Suto, 148
Sutu, 132, 136
Suundi, 56, 59, 60
Swahili, 115, 121, 126–9
Swaka, 80, 82
Swäsë, 3, 5

Swati, Swazi, 138, 151, 152, 153, 154
Sweta, 113, 114
Swina, 143
Swɔsə, 3
Syan, 105

Taabwa, 80–81
Tabara, 145
Tabele, 152
Tabwa, 80
Taconi, Tadjoni, 111, 112
Tagwenda, 105, 108
Taita, 115, 125, 129
Takama, 119
Takwenda, 105
Talahundra, 144
Talinga, Talinge, 105, 108
Tambo, 77, 78, 137, 138
Tambuka, 137
Tande, 143
Tanga, 9
Tangi, 95, 96
Tatsoni, 111
Taųŋ, Taung, 148, 150
Tavara, 145
Taveta, 122
Tavhatsindi, 147
Tawana, 148, 149
Tcengui, Tchangui, 27
Tebe, 144
Tebele, 152
Tege, Tégué, 29
Teita, 125
Teke, 27, 29–31, 51
Tekela, Tekeza, 152, 153
Tembo¹ (Ngombe Gr.), 43, 44
Tembo² (Samba-Holu Gr.), 65
Tembo³ (Tambo), 77, 138
Tembo⁴ (Shi-Hunde Gr.), 97, 98
Tende¹ (Tįini), 29
Tende² (Kurja), 113
Teo, 29
Teri, 125
Teta, 139
Tetela, Tetɛla, 49, 51, 52–53
[Terik, 112]
Teve, Teʋe, 144
Tharaka, Tharaka, 115, 125
Thembu, 152, 153
Thlapįŋ, Thlaping, 148, 150
Thlaro, Thlaru, 148, 150
Thonga, 155
Tiene, Tįini, 29, 31
Tike, 89, 90
Tikulu, Tikuu, 126, 127
Timbuka, 137
Tindi, 111
Tio, 29
Tiriki, 111, 112
Tįtụ, Titu, 48, 49

Tjimba, 160
Tlapi, 148
Tlokoa, Tlokwa, 149, 150, 151
Tofoke, 46
Toka, 83, 84
Tokwa, 149
Tombucas, 137
Tonga¹ (Ila Gr.), 83–84
Tonga² (Manda Gr.), 136, 137, 138
Tonga³ (Nyanja Gr.), 139, 140
Tonga⁴ (Nsenga Gr.), 141
Tonga⁵ (Shona Gr.), 144
Tonga⁶ (Chopi Gr.), 157
Tonga⁷ (Tsonga), 155
Tongwe, 118
Tooro, 105, 108
Topoke, 46
Toro, 105
Totela, 83–84, 85
Tsaam, Tsaamba, 57, 61
Tsaangi, 27
Tsaayi, 29, 30
Tsangi, 27
Tsaye, Tsayi, 29
Tschokwe, 67
Tschopi, 157
Tshiboko, 67
Tshiga, 104, 107
Tshiluba, 72
Tshiok, 67
Tshobwa, 54
Tshogo, 104, 107
Tsogo, 25
Tsonga, 155–6
Tsotso¹ (Kongo Gr.), 58
Tsotso², Tsootso, 111, 112
Tsunga, Tsuŋga, 143
Tswa, 155, 156
Tswana, Tšwana, 148, 149–50
Tswena, Tsweni, 148–50
Tubeta, 122
Tukkongo, Tukongo, 54
Tukulu, 126
Tukungu, 54
Tumba, 139, 140
Tumbatu, 126, 127
Tumboka, Tumbuka, 78, 136, 137–8
Tumbwe, 92, 93
Tungu, 43
Turumbu, 62
Tusi, Tussi, Tutsi, 106–7
Twa, 104, 107
Tyo, 29

Umbundu, 158
Unguja, 126, 127–8
Unyama, 144
Upoto, 38, 41
Ururagwe, 105
Ushi, Usi, Uzhi, 80

Vanuma, 101
Veiao, 134
Venda, Veṇḍa, 147
Vidunda, 123, 124
Vili[1] (Njabi Gr.), 27
Vili[2] (Kongo Gr.), 57, 60
Vinza, 100
Vira, 92, 94
'Vita' Swahili, 128
Vumba, 126, 127
Vungunya, 57, 60

Waganga, 139
Wajao, 134
Wanda, Wandia, 77
Wandji, 27
Wanga, 111
Wangata, 48, 49
Wanji, 131
Ware, 113, 114
We, 83, 84
Wemba, 80
Wenya, 137, 138
Wiinza-Baali, 43
Wisa, 80
Wongo, Wongo, 54, 55
Wouri, 7
Woyo, 57
Wụmbvụ, 24
Wumu, 29
Wunjo, 117
Wuõ, 30
Wuri, 7
Wuumu, 29, 30

Xaayo, 111, 112
Xananwa, 148, 150
Xesibe, 152, 153

Xhosa, 152, 153, 154
Xikongo, 56
Xinji, 57
Xosa, 152

Yaa, 29, 30
Yaamba, 48, 50
Yabasi, 10, 11
Yaikole, 50
Yailima, 48, 49
Yaisu, 48, 50
Yajima, 48
Yaka[1] (Kakɔ), 22
Yaka[2] (Yaa), 29
Yaka[3] (Kongo Gr.), 57, 58, 60, 61
Yalihila, 50
Yalikandja, 50
Yalikoka, 46, 47
Yambasa, 14
Yambeta, 10, 12
Yamongeri, 42
Yana, 70
Yangafĕk, Yaŋgafuk, 16, 17
Yangonda, 50
Yanongo, 47
Yans, Yansi, Yanzi, 29, 31
Yao, 134
Yaokandja, 46, 47
Yasa, 9
Yaşem, 16, 17
Yaunde, 16–18
Yawembe, 46, 47
Yebanda, 18
Yeei[1] (Teke-Yans Gr.), 29, 31
Yeei[2], Yei[1], 160
Yei[2] (Luyana Gr.), 70, 71
Yekaba, 17
Yela, Yela, 52, 53
Yelinda, 18

Yembama, 18
Yembani, 18
Yembe[1] (Kongo Gr.), 58, 62
Yembe[2] (Songe), 72
Yengong, 18
Yengono, 18
Yesoum, 16
Yetchoa, 18
Yewu, 43, 45
Yey, 29
Yeye, Yeyi, 160
Yezum, Yezum, 16
Yira, 95, 97
Yiru, 105
Yoa, Yoba, 98
Yombe[1], Yombɛ (Kongo Gr.), 57, 60
Yombe[2] (Tumbuka), 137, 138
Yongo, 65
Yoza, 104

Zaman, 18
Zanaki, 113, 114
Zarano, 123-4
Zeguha, 122
Zezuru, 143
Ziba[1] (Shi-Hunde Gr.), 97
Ziba[2] (Inter-Lacustrine Gr.), 104, 106
Ziba[3] (Dzindza), 104
Zigua, Zigula, 122, 123
Zimba, 143
Zịmba, 92, 93
Zimu, 19
Zinja, Zinza, 104, 106
Ziraha, 123
Zombo, Zoombo, 56, 59
Zulu, Zunda, 153, 154
Zyoba, 92, 94

For Product Safety Concerns and Information please contact our EU
representative GPSR@taylorandfrancis.com
Taylor & Francis Verlag GmbH, Kaufingerstraße 24, 80331 München, Germany

www.ingramcontent.com/pod-product-compliance
Lightning Source LLC
Chambersburg PA
CBHW052125300426
44116CB00010B/1790